# 1 Peter, 2 Peter, and Jude

TEACHING CHRIST IN ALL OF SCRIPTURE

*Head, Heart,*
*Hand Bible Studies*

Ezra and Nehemiah — *The Good Hand of Our God Is upon Us*

Isaiah — *The Holy One of Israel*

Luke — *That You May Have Certainty concerning the Faith*

Romans — *The Gospel of God for Obedience to the Faith*

1 Peter, 2 Peter, and Jude — *Steadfast in the Faith*

# 1 Peter, 2 Peter, and Jude

*Steadfast in the Faith*

Sarah Ivill

**Reformation Heritage Books**

Grand Rapids, Michigan

**Reformation Heritage Books**
3070 29th St. SE
Grand Rapids, MI 49512
616-977-0889
orders@heritagebooks.org
www.heritagebooks.org

*Printed in the United States of America*
22 23 24 25 26 27/10 9 8 7 6 5 4 3

Library of Congress Cataloging-in-Publication Data

Names: Ivill, Sarah, author.
Title: 1 Peter, 2 Peter, and Jude : steadfast in the faith / Sarah Ivill.
Other titles: First Peter, second Peter, and Jude
Description: Grand Rapids, Michigan : Reformation Heritage Books, 2017. | Includes bibliographical references.
Identifiers: LCCN 2016057920 (print) | LCCN 2017001410 (ebook) | ISBN 9781601785244 (pbk. : alk. paper) | ISBN 9781601785251 (epub)
Subjects: LCSH: Bible. Peter–Textbooks. | Bible. Jude–Textbooks.
Classification: LCC BS2795.55 .I95 2017 (print) | LCC BS2795.55 (ebook) | DDC 227/.9207–dc23
LC record available at https://lccn.loc.gov/2016057920

*For additional Reformed literature, request a free book list from Reformation Heritage Books at the above regular or e-mail address.*

*To my heavenly Father, who, according to His great mercy, has caused me to be born again to a living hope through the resurrection of Jesus Christ from the dead, to an inheritance that is imperishable, undefiled, and unfading, kept in heaven for me, who by God's power is being guarded through faith for a salvation ready to be revealed in the last time.*

—from 1 PETER 1:3–5

❖ ❖ ❖ ❖

*To the One whose divine power has given to us all things that pertain to life and godliness, through the knowledge of Him who called us by glory and virtue, by which have been given to us exceedingly great and precious promises, that through these we may be partakers of the divine nature, having escaped the corruption that is in the world through lust.*

—from 2 PETER 1:3–4

❖ ❖ ❖ ❖

*To Him who is able to keep us from stumbling and to present us faultless before the presence of His glory with exceeding joy, to God our Savior, who alone is wise, be glory and majesty, dominion and power, both now and forevermore.*

—from JUDE 24–25

# Contents

# Foreword

Once again Sarah Ivill has combined serious scholarly study with evangelical piety and gospel application to produce a helpful study for women (and men) who may use this book to study Peter and Jude. In my own preaching, I have a growing appreciation for these three small epistles at the end of our New Testament that were written at the end of the apostolic age. We live in a world of falsehood, of militant immorality, and of brazen irreverence for Christ and the things of God. Sarah will challenge us all to deal with these three strands of soul poison not by skirting around tough subjects or difficult problems, but by leaning into Jesus Christ and applying His word to our lives. I commend this study of 1 and 2 Peter and Jude to all who seek a soul tonic for a godless age.

—Michael F. Ross, Senior Pastor
Christ Covenant Church
Matthews, North Carolina

# A Note from Sarah

Many women today are drowning in despair, flailing their arms in futility, and sinking in seas of sin and suffering. They reach out to false, futile saviors, clinging to things or relationships that are as capable of saving them as sticks floating in the sea and the wind that crashes with each wave. This is tragic, especially because the lifeboat that could secure them to the heaviest anchor is right in front of them. But they continue to try to save themselves, shirking the secure way.

Perhaps no one has told them that the lifeboat, the Word of God, is their very life, because it reveals Jesus Christ, the anchor of their souls and the One to whom all Scripture points. Only as women are saturated in the Scriptures that point them to the Savior will they swim in hope, surf waves in security, and stand on shore anchored to the truth.

Let us return to being women of one Book above all others. If you have time to read only one book, make it Scripture. Then, if you have time to read more, you will be well trained to tell the difference between what merely tickles your ears and what mightily transforms your heart.

My love for teaching the Word of God was inspired by my own hunger to study it. Longing for the meat of God's Word and finding it lacking in so many churches today, I enrolled in Bible Study Fellowship after graduating from high school. It was there that I realized my desire to attend seminary and was influenced and encouraged by a strong godly woman and mentor to attend Dallas Theological Seminary (DTS). During this time I was leading women through Bible studies and caught a glimpse of how much they desired to be fed God's Word in depth. This encouraged me even further to receive an education that would best prepare me to deliver God's Word to women who hungered for the truth.

Upon graduating with my Master of Theology from DTS, I took a position as assistant director of women's ministry at a large church where I served under a woman who shared my passion to teach the meat of God's Word. Within the year, I had assumed the role of director and delved into teaching the Word of God in an expository and applicable manner. After three years I resigned in order to stay home with my first child. During those years at home, the Lord used my experience in seminary and ministry to lead me back to my roots and the full embracing of Reformed theology. Raised for the first half of my childhood in conservative Presbyterian churches, I had been grounded in the Reformed faith and catechisms from an early age. But from middle school on, I was not in Reformed churches. The question in my twenties then became, What do I really believe?

One of the first steps on my journey was contacting a Reformed seminary and asking for a list of books covering everything I had missed by not attending a Reformed seminary. That began my reading of some of the most renowned Reformed theologians in the world. It was during those days that the question of what I really believed was finally answered, and I began teaching women based on my understanding of Reformed theology. In fact, that is how my first Bible study came to be written. I had the incredible privilege of teaching that first study to a wonderful group of women for a morning Bible study at the church we were then attending. And it was from their encouragement and exhortation that I submitted the study for publication.

I want to encourage you as you embark upon the study of 1 Peter, 2 Peter, and Jude. As you read, ponder what the Word of God has to say about the depth of our sin and the judgment we deserve, and rejoice at the wonders of grace and salvation. In every chapter keep your eyes on Jesus, the One to whom all Scripture points, and worship Him for the work of salvation that He has accomplished for you through the power of the Holy Spirit, to the glory of God the Father. *Soli Deo gloria!*

# Acknowledgments

I wish to thank those in my life who have been a part of this writing process.

Thank you to Reformation Heritage Books, especially Jay Collier for his interest in this project and Annette Gysen for her graciousness, hard work, and many excellent suggestions. This was a team effort!

Thank you to the pastors, especially Michael F. Ross for writing the foreword, and the women of Christ Covenant Church (PCA) who have been a part of this process and who have encouraged me to keep writing Bible studies for women.

Thank you to the men and women of Dallas Theological Seminary who taught me what it means to be a gracious student of Scripture and who instilled in me the importance of expository teaching and the love of God's Word.

Thank you to Westminster Theological Seminary and the professors who have served there. The many books that have been written and recommended by the professors, as well as the many online class lectures and chapel messages, have been of tremendous benefit to me. They have taught me what it means to see Christ in all of Scripture and to understand more deeply the history of redemption and the beautiful truths of Reformed theology.

Thank you to my many dear friends (you know who you are!) who prayed for me and encouraged me to make the dream of writing a reality.

Thank you to my mom and dad, who have always supported me in my love of the Word and encouraged me to do that which the Lord has called me to do. I love you both more than words can express.

Thank you to my husband, Charles, who has always given me his love, support, and encouragement in the writing process and in what the Lord has called me to do.

And thank you to my children, Caleb, Hannah, Daniel, and Lydia, whose sweet smiles, loving hugs, prayers for "Mom's Bible studies," and patience as I "finish another thought" before tending to one of their many needs are a constant source of encouragement to me as I pray for the next generation of believers to love the Lord and His Word with all their hearts and minds.

Finally, thank you to my heavenly Father, to my Lord and Savior Jesus Christ, and to the Spirit, who helps me in my weakness. To the triune God be the glory for what He has done through me, a broken vessel and a flawed instrument, yet one that is in the grip of His mighty and gracious hand.

# Introduction to This Study

It is my sincere hope that you are excited about studying Scripture, particularly the books of 1 Peter, 2 Peter, and Jude. It is also my sincere desire that this study will help fuel your excitement. In this introduction I have provided three resources that I hope prove beneficial to you. First, I have provided an overview of how to use this Bible study. Feel free to adapt my suggestions to the context in which you will be using this study. I want this study to be a help to you, not a hindrance!

Second, I have provided an overview of the history of redemption and revelation. When we study Scripture, it is sometimes easy to get so focused on the original context that we forget to pull back and study a passage with regard to its redemptive-historical context (which considers the question of where we are in salvation history). I hope this overview gives you a sense of the overarching story of Scripture.

Finally, I have provided an overview of what it means to study Christ in all of Scripture. You may wonder why this is necessary for books like 1 Peter, 2 Peter, and Jude, but as I will explain later, people often teach these books in a legalistic or moralistic way, focusing more on what we are to do than on what Christ has already done for us. It is crucial we connect the passages to Christ first, so that we understand our salvation is by grace alone through faith alone.

## How to Use this Bible Study

This study is organized into four main parts:

(1) *Purpose:* This brief section introduces you to the passage you will be studying and is meant to guide you into how the lesson applies to your head (knowledge about God), your heart (affection for God), and your hands (service for God). Although it is brief, this is a significant section to read since it tells you in a nutshell what the lesson is all about, giving you the big picture before studying the finer details.

(2) *Personal Study:* This section of questions is meant to help you dig deeply into God's Word so that you might be equipped to worship God, work for His kingdom purposes, and witness for Him to a watching world. To assist you in your study, you may want to have a good study Bible and concordance close at hand. I would encourage

you to not get overwhelmed by the questions, or think you have to answer every one of them, but to relax and enjoy the study of God's Word.

(3) *Putting It All Together.* This section is meant to help answer any lingering questions you may still have after your personal study time and assist you in tying things together from the lesson questions. I highly recommend you read this section, especially if you are preparing to lead a group of women through this study. Regardless of whether you are leading or participating in the study, this section will prove helpful in cementing in your mind everything you've previously studied and will better prepare you to process things together with your Bible study group.

(4) *Processing It Together.* This section of questions is meant to help you study the Word of God in the context of community, sharing what you have learned from God's Word together so that you might sharpen one another, encourage one another, and pray for one another. Group leaders: Ideally, the women have worked through the previous three sections before coming together as a group. Your first gathering might be a time of fellowship and a discussion of the introduction to the book. Then you can assign the ladies the homework for the first lesson. Encourage them to read the purpose, work through the personal study questions, and read through "Putting It All Together." Remind them to relax and enjoy the study, encouraging them to come to the group time regardless of whether their homework is complete. You may want to star certain questions from your personal study that you want to cover in the group time, as well as highlight any sections from "Putting It All Together" to discuss. I would recommend reviewing the "Purpose" at the beginning of your group time as well. Don't forget to begin and end with prayer and to foster a warm and inviting environment where women can grow together in thinking biblically, being anchored in the truth, and living covenantally, being anchored in the covenant community.

Now that we have taken a look at how this study is organized, let's turn our attention to the big story of the Bible so that we might have a better grasp of the bigger context in which 1 Peter, 2 Peter, and Jude fit.

## An Overview of the History of Redemption and Revelation

God has chosen to enter into a covenant relationship with His people. He is the covenant King; we are the covenant servants. As our covenant King, He acts in history, bringing about both His word and His works. As His covenant servants, we are to obey His word.

It is only in Christ that the covenant King and the covenant servants meet. Christ is both the Lord of the covenant and the Servant of the covenant. He has come as the Lord of the covenant to extend grace and mercy to God's rebellious servants, and He has come as the Servant of the covenant to perfectly fulfill what God's people could never do, thus bringing blessing to all those who place their faith in Him.

Amazingly, our covenant King has chosen to dwell among His people. Throughout redemptive history we see a progression of God dwelling with His people. First, we observe Him dwelling with Adam and Eve in the garden. Then we see Him meet with His people in the tabernacle and then the temple and dwell with them there. But the climax is when Jesus came to earth and tabernacled among us, fulfilling God's promise, "I will take you as My people, and I will be your God" (Ex. 6:7). When Christ returns He will consummately fulfill this promise as we dwell with the triune God in the new heaven and the new earth forever (Rev. 21:3).

If we are to understand the overarching story of Scripture, we need to recognize the different covenants in the history of redemption: the covenant of redemption, the covenant of works, and the covenant of grace. What theologians call the *covenant of redemption* is described in Ephesians 1:4, which teaches us that God the Father chose us in Christ "before the foundation of the world, that we should be holy and without blame before Him." The Father has purposed our redemption, the Son has accomplished it, and the Holy Spirit applies it.

In Genesis 1–2 we learn of God's covenant with Adam before the fall. This covenant established a relationship between the Creator and the creature that involved *worship* (keeping the Sabbath day holy), *work* (ruling and multiplying), *woman* (marriage and procreation), and the *word of God* (God gave Adam a command when He put him in the garden of Eden to work it and keep it. He could eat of any tree in the garden except one, the tree of the knowledge of good and evil. God told Adam that if he ate of that tree he would die; if he obeyed, he would live). Theologians refer to this pre-fall covenant with Adam as the *covenant of works*, the *covenant of life*, or the *covenant of creation*.

Tragically, Adam failed to obey, and all mankind fell with him in this first sin. But God sounds a note of grace in Genesis 3:15: death will not have the final word. In His post-fall covenant with Adam, God promises that He will put enmity between the serpent and the woman, between the serpent's offspring and the woman's offspring. The woman's offspring would bruise the serpent's head, and the serpent would bruise His heel. This is the gospel in seed form. Ultimately, the woman's offspring is Christ. Christ defeated sin and death on the cross, triumphing over all His enemies.

Along with God's blessed promise to the woman that she would continue to produce *seed*, or offspring, the greatest of which is Christ, He also told her that she would experience the curse of *sorrow* with regard to children and the curse of *struggle* with regard to her husband.

God spoke a word to Adam also. He promised the man that he would receive the blessing of *sustenance*. But he would also experience the curse of *sweaty toil* and the *separation of soul and body* in death. Theologians call this post-fall covenant the *covenant of grace*. Titus 3:4–7 provides a good summary of this covenant: "But when the kindness and the love of God our Savior toward man appeared, not by works of righteousness which we have done, but according to His mercy He saved us, through the washing of regeneration and renewing of the Holy Spirit, whom He poured out on us abundantly through Jesus Christ our Savior, that having been justified by His grace we should become heirs according to the hope of eternal life." The covenant of grace includes

God's post-fall covenant with Adam (Gen. 3:15), Noah (Gen. 6:17–22; 8:20–22; 9:1–17), Abraham (Gen. 12:1–3; 15:1–20; 17:1–2), Moses (Exodus 19–24 and Deuteronomy), and David (2 Samuel 7), as well as the new covenant, all of which are fulfilled in Jesus Christ (Jer. 31:31–34). Let's take a closer look now at each of these covenants, as well as some other important events that were occurring in redemptive history, so that we have a better grasp of the story of salvation.

After the note of the gospel of grace is sounded to Adam and Eve in Genesis 3:15, we learn of God's covenant with Noah recorded in Genesis 9. The Lord promises that as long as the earth remains, seedtime and harvest, cold and heat, summer and winter, and day and night will continue. This is amazing grace, for it promises that there will be an earth on which the history of salvation will unfold. Just think if there had been no day for Jesus to be born in Bethlehem or to die on the cross!

God's covenant with Noah also promises that though the righteous will be saved, the wicked will be judged, a theme that is predominant all through Scripture. God's original purposes of worship, work, and woman in the pre-fall covenant with Adam are renewed in the context of the history of redemption. God's covenant with Noah can be summarized by the following: God's *glorious grace* alongside His *glorious justice*; the *genealogical aspect* of the covenant (God will deal with families, not just individuals); the *goodness* of life; and the *general grace* extended to all mankind, including the universe. The sign of this covenant, the rainbow, is most appropriate, then, as it shines God's grace in the midst of the cloudy storm of judgment.

In Genesis 12, 15, and 22, we learn of God's covenant with Abraham, which is later renewed with Isaac and Jacob. First, God promises His *presence*. The crux of the covenant of grace can be summed up in one phrase, "I will walk among you and be your God, and you shall be My people" (Lev. 26:12). Second, God promises Abraham a *people*; God would make him a great nation. Third, God promises Abraham a *possession*; He would give His people the land of Canaan. Fourth, God promises Abraham that he has a bigger *purpose* than he could ever imagine. The nation that came through his seed was to point others to the Lord so that all the families of the earth would be blessed.

In Exodus, we learn of God's covenant with Moses, the mediator of the law the Lord made with Israel, which can be summarily comprehended in the Ten Commandments. This is the beginning of the theocratic nation of Israel.[1] God brought His people out of slavery in Egypt and into a relationship with Him as servants of the holy God. As such, they were to be a kingdom of priests and a holy nation (Ex. 19:6). We learn in both Leviticus 26 and Deuteronomy 28 that if they were obedient, they would receive blessings (Lev. 26:1–13; Deut. 28:1–14), but if they were disobedient, they would receive curses (Lev. 26:14–46; Deut. 28:15–68). One of these curses, the greatest, was exile from the land. But even toward the end of Deuteronomy, we see that God

---

1. By a theocratic nation, I mean that Israel's earthly kings, priests, and prophets recognized God as the true King, and as such served to interpret and enforce His laws for the people.

made provision for restoration after the exile, which involved the new covenant (Deut. 30:1–10; see also Jer. 31:31–34; Ezek. 37:21, 26).

In fact, Deuteronomy 28–30 is the CliffsNotes version of the rest of the Old Testament. First comes blessing, climaxing in the reign of King Solomon (1 Kings 8:24). Then come curses, ultimately resulting in exile from the land (2 Chron. 36:17–21). All the prophets refer to the covenant blessings and curses as they prophesy to Israel and Judah, giving them messages of judgment as well as holding out the hope of blessing. Though the prophets declare that exile is inevitable, they also declare God's faithfulness to His covenant, keeping the promise of the new covenant before them (Deut. 30:1–10; Jer. 31:31–34; Ezek. 37:21, 26).

After Moses died, the Lord raised up Joshua to lead the people into the promised land, which was the place where God would dwell with His people in the temple. Up to this point in redemptive history, the garden of Eden and the tabernacle had been the places the Lord had temporarily dwelt with His people. The entire book of Joshua centers on the entry into and conquest of the land.

But then Joshua died, and in the book of Judges we see that the people failed to conquer the land as they should have. Instead, they did what was right in their own eyes, because there was no king in Israel. The books of Judges and Ruth anticipate the beginning of the monarchy in Israel with King Saul and King David.

In 2 Samuel 7, God makes a covenant with David concerning an eternal kingdom with an eternal Davidic king. First, God promises David a *position*, taking him from being a shepherd of sheep to making him a shepherd king over his people with a great name. Second, God promises David a *place*. Israel would be planted in their own place. Third, God promises David *peace*. In their own place, Israel would have rest from their enemies. Finally, God promises David *progeny*. The Lord would raise up David's offspring and establish His kingdom forever.

The period of the monarchy climaxes in King Solomon, when the promises are fulfilled in Solomon's prayer of dedication (1 Kings 8:24). Sadly, it didn't take long (within Solomon's reign) for the monarchy to take a turn for the worse (1 Kings 11). Following Solomon's death, the country actually divided into the Northern Kingdom (Israel) and the Southern Kingdom (Judah) in 931 BC (1 Kings 12:16–24).

Elijah and Elisha preached to the Northern Kingdom during this time. Although there were a few good kings, the majority of kings in both Israel and Judah did evil in the sight of the Lord and led the people into rebellion as well. In His grace and mercy, God raised up prophets during this time to prophesy to the people of coming judgment so that they would turn and repent of their wicked ways. Hosea and Amos preached to the Northern Kingdom, while Isaiah and Micah preached to the Southern Kingdom. Joel, Obadiah, and Jonah also preached their messages during this time. Tragically, the Northern Kingdom did not listen and was taken into captivity by the Assyrians in 722 BC.

A little over one hundred years later, the same thing happened to the Southern Kingdom, except it was the Babylonians who took them into captivity. This involved three different deportations in 605, 597, and 586 BC. In the second of these deportations, Jehoiachin, the last true Davidic king on the throne, was taken, along with the royal family and all the leading classes in Israel, to Babylon. God's promises seemed to be thwarted.

But again, in God's mercy, He raised up both Daniel and Ezekiel to prophesy to the people during the exile (Jeremiah was still prophesying during this time as well). Daniel and Ezekiel spoke messages of both judgment and restoration to the exiles. God would still be faithful to His covenant promise; He would be their God, and they would be His people. Both Jeremiah and Ezekiel spoke of the promised new covenant (Jer. 31:31–34; Ezek. 37:21, 26), inaugurated by Christ during the last Passover, which was also the first Lord's Supper, with His disciples before His death.

The new covenant involved seven different promises. First, God promised His people would *return* to the land of promise. Second, God promised a *restoration of the land.* Third, God promised a *realization of each of His previous promises* to Adam, Noah, Abraham, Moses, and David. Fourth, God promised a *renewed heart.* Fifth, God promised the *removal of sin.* Sixth, God promised a *reunion of Israel and Judah under one ruler,* Jesus Christ. Finally, God promised the *realization of redemption* (this was the final covenant, and, as such, it secured redemption).

Following the exile, God raised up the prophets Haggai, Zechariah, and Malachi to continue speaking to His people. Though there is a small fulfillment of a restored temple, people, and land under the leadership of Zerubbabel and Nehemiah, the promises of God could not be completely fulfilled until Jesus Christ came. As Paul so eloquently says, "All the promises of God in Him are Yes, and in Him Amen, to the glory of God through us" (2 Cor. 1:20).

The Gospels record for us the amazing truth of the incarnation. Jesus came to earth as a baby, lived a life of perfect obedience, died for the sins of God's people, was raised as the firstfruits of the resurrection, and ascended to the Father. Acts 2 records that the Holy Spirit was sent on the day of Pentecost to renew the church and establish it by His power.

The new age was inaugurated through Christ and His church, but it awaits its consummation until Christ returns to bring the old age to a complete end with the final judgment and usher in the new heaven and the new earth. In the meantime, the church is to fulfill the Great Commission: "And Jesus came and spoke to them, saying, 'All authority has been given to Me in heaven and on earth. Go therefore and make disciples of all the nations, baptizing them in the name of the Father and of the Son and of the Holy Spirit, teaching them to observe all things that I have commanded you; and lo, I am with you always, even to the end of the age.' Amen" (Matt. 28:18–20; see also Luke 24:47–49).

As we study any passage of Scripture, it is important for us to keep this overview of the history of redemption and revelation in mind. After studying the original context of the passage, we must ask the question, How does this text relate to the history of redemption? In other words, where is it in progressive, redemptive history? Then we must ask, How does this text relate to the climax of redemptive history, the life, death, resurrection, and ascension of our Lord and Savior Jesus Christ? The latter question leads us to the next section we need to consider in order to teach Christ in all of Scripture.

## A Christ-Centered Interpretation of 1 Peter, 2 Peter, and Jude

The story of Jesus begins in the Old Testament, in the opening chapters of Genesis, with the account of creation. As the apostle John so eloquently says, "In the beginning was the Word, and the Word was with God, and the Word was God. He was in the beginning with God. All things were made through Him, and without Him nothing was made that was made. In Him was life, and the life was the light of men. And the light shines in the darkness, and the darkness did not comprehend it" (John 1:1–5). Paul echoes this truth in Colossians 1:15–17: "He is the image of the invisible God, the firstborn over all creation. For by Him all things were created that are in heaven and that are on earth, visible and invisible, whether thrones or dominions or principalities or powers. All things were created through Him and for Him. And He is before all things, and in Him all things consist."

Matthew, like John, doesn't begin his gospel account with the birth of Jesus; rather, he opens with the genealogy of Jesus Christ, reaching all the way back through the Old Testament to Abraham. In chapter 3 of his gospel, Luke goes back even further, tracing the story of Jesus all the way to Adam, the son of God. Paul too traces the story of Jesus back to Adam when he says, "And so it is written, 'The first man Adam became a living being.' The last Adam became a life-giving spirit" (1 Cor. 15:45). Even before the fall, the first man Adam pointed forward to the greater and final Adam, Jesus Christ. Luke closes his gospel with Jesus's own account of His story, so since we are learning about Him from Him, we should pay close attention as we read His words in Luke 24.

Two disciples were trying to put together the story of Jesus. They had been in Jerusalem and witnessed the events at the end of Jesus's life. They had seven long miles to try to figure it out as they journeyed from Jerusalem to Emmaus, but they couldn't understand. In fact, they were deeply distressed. Their hope had been deflated. They thought that He was the one to redeem Israel, but instead He was crucified and buried. Indeed, the tomb was empty, but Jesus was nowhere to be seen.

Note carefully what Jesus says to them: "'O foolish ones, and slow of heart to believe in all that the prophets have spoken! Ought not the Christ to have suffered these things and to enter into His glory?' And beginning at Moses and all the Prophets, He expounded to them in all the Scriptures the things concerning Himself" (Luke 24:25–27).

Wouldn't you have liked to walk those seven miles with the three of them? It was the greatest walk those disciples would have in their entire lives as the Master Teacher told His own story, beginning in Genesis and moving all the way through the Prophets. It was the privilege not only of these two Emmaus disciples but also the disciples who had been with Him during His earthly ministry to hear Jesus tell His story. Luke tells us later in the same chapter that Jesus opened their minds to understand the Scriptures, everything written about Him in the Law of Moses and the Prophets and the Psalms. These things had to be fulfilled, and Jesus was telling them that He was the fulfillment (Luke 24:44–47).

He is the second Adam who did not sin but was obedient to death on the cross. He is the seed of the woman who crushed the serpent's head. He is the final Noah who saved His people through the cross. He is the final Abraham in whom all the families of the earth are blessed. He is the final Isaac who was sacrificed for our sin. He is the true Israel who was tested and tried in the wilderness and obeyed. He is the greater and final Moses who has been counted worthy of more honor since He is faithful over God's house as a son. He is the final judge who never did what was right in His own eyes or fell into sin but delivered His people by taking their judgment for them. He is the final prophet who suffered for His people and did so without opening His mouth in retaliation. He is the final priest who has offered Himself as the final sacrifice to atone for our sins. He is the final psalmist who leads His people in praise to God. He is the final Davidic king who reigns in perfect justice and righteousness. He is the final Solomon who is not only full of wisdom but is wisdom Himself (1 Cor. 1:30).

Peter is proof that Jesus opened His disciples' minds to understand that day, for in Acts 2 we read his sermon, which he begins by citing David's words in Psalm 16:8–11 and ends by citing his words in Psalm 110:1. He speaks these words in between:

> Men and brethren, let me speak freely to you of the patriarch David, that he is both dead and buried, and his tomb is with us to this day. Therefore, being a prophet, and knowing that God had sworn with an oath to him that of the fruit of his body, according to the flesh, He would raise up the Christ to sit on his throne, he, foreseeing this, spoke concerning the resurrection of the Christ, that His soul was not left in Hades, nor did His flesh see corruption. This Jesus God has raised up, of which we are all witnesses. Therefore being exalted at the right hand of God, and having received from the Father the promise of the Holy Spirit, He poured out this which you now see and hear. (Acts 2:29–33)

We cannot tell the story of Jesus in any way we please. We must learn from Jesus Himself and tell the story beginning with Genesis and Deuteronomy, moving through the Prophets and the Psalms, and then the New Testament Gospels and Letters, closing with Revelation, where the end of the story is told: "Now I saw a new heaven and a new earth, for the first heaven and the first earth had passed away" (Rev. 21:1). The end of the story isn't really the end, for we will spend an eternity worshiping Him "who is and who was and who is to come,… Jesus Christ, the faithful witness, the firstborn from the dead, and the ruler over the kings of the earth," the One who loves us and has freed us from our sins by His blood and "has made us kings and priests to His God and Father" (Rev. 1:4–6).

We have looked at some key texts, so now let's look at some key phrases for identifying the continuity between the Old and New Testaments. We might say that we go from Old Testament promise to New Testament fulfillment, or from Old Testament problem (sinners in need of a Savior) to New Testament solution (the Savior comes), or from Old Testament anticipation to New Testament realization, but not just a realization—a far-surpassing realization. For example, Jesus Christ is not just a greater Moses, Samson, prophet, priest, or king, but the greatest and final Moses, Samson, prophet, priest, and king. Furthermore, the Lord of history designs historical persons, offices, institutions, and events to foreshadow the full redemption to come. Thus, He foreshadows His great work of redemption in both words and works (events).[2]

The climax in all of Scripture is the gospel—the life, death, resurrection, and ascension of Jesus Christ. All the Old Testament writers look toward this climax. All the New Testament writers look both back to this climax and forward to the consummation of the kingdom, Christ's second coming, which was inaugurated at His first coming. There are really four main questions, then, when we are studying Scripture: (1) What is the original context of this passage? (2) Where are we in the history of redemption in this text? (3) How does this text relate to the gospel? (4) How do I apply this text to my life right now in light of where I am in redemptive history?

These questions keep us from a legalistic reading of the text ("Do this, and you will live"), a moralistic reading of the text ("Be a good person, and you will be saved"), a therapeutic reading of the text ("I'm good, you're good, God is good, everything is okay"), and an allegorical reading of the text ("I'm going to make this text refer to Christ no matter what interpretive principles I have to break!"). Instead, we will be women who glean a Christ-centered message.

---

2. Dennis Johnson, *Him We Proclaim: Preaching Christ from All the Scriptures* (Phillipsburg, N.J.: P&R, 2007), 225–26.

# 1 Peter

## The True Grace of God

# Introduction to 1 Peter

Judeo-Christian values are under assault in our culture today, leaving many people grappling with questions that are not new: Who am I? How do I find peace? Is there any hope? If God cares about me, why am I suffering? What is the gospel? Is Jesus more than a good moral teacher? Does holiness matter, and, if so, how do I become holy? Is God my judge, my friend, or both? How do I love someone who causes me so much pain? Does becoming a Christian mean I have to say good-bye to my old friends? Does going to church really matter, or is Christianity just about me and my relationship with God? If I am saved by grace, do good deeds really matter? What does submission have to do with the twenty-first century? What is true freedom? How do I suffer for the glory of God? If God is sovereign, does prayer really matter? Is the power- and prestige-hungry pastor/teacher/speaker really a problem? Is the devil real, and, if so, how should I think of him?

Furthermore, the gospel is under assault in our churches today, leaving many people arguing over definitions of the true grace of God. Peter's first letter, though originally written for a different time and place, bridges the time gap between the centuries, speaking powerfully to both the culture's and the church's current issues. Peter declares the true grace of God and exhorts us to stand firm in it. We are in desperate need of Peter's message today, for it is God's message to you and me for such a time as this.

## The Author, Date, and Audience of 1 Peter

The divine author of Scripture is God Himself: "All Scripture is given by inspiration of God, and is profitable for doctrine, for reproof, for correction, for instruction in righteousness, that the man of God may be complete, thoroughly equipped for every good work" (2 Tim. 3:16–17). But the Holy Spirit used human authors to speak and write the Word of God (2 Peter 1:21).

3

The human author of the book of 1 Peter is the apostle Peter. Saved on the shores of the sea, Peter responded to Jesus's call to follow Him. What a journey it was for Peter! The fisherman never could have told you how much impatience, pride, selfishness, evil, and faithlessness would be rooted out of him as he followed Christ. But through the Gospels, and into the book of Acts, and finally with 1 and 2 Peter, we see a transformation take place that can be attributed only to the grace of God. Peter witnessed Jesus's life, death, resurrection, and ascension. He learned at the Master's feet. He knew Christ's forgiveness and grace after denial. And he knew the suffering that came by being Christ's follower and a leader in the early church. The story of Peter is one I love, for it shines the spotlight on our Savior. Peter's life tells us we don't have to have it together in order to be saved; rather, God saves us in order to put us together.

The book of 1 Peter was most likely written in AD 62–63, and this date is based on events in both Paul's and Peter's lives. New Testament scholars D. A. Carson and Douglas J. Moo believe that the apostle Paul was probably not in Rome when Peter wrote this letter, having left after he was released from an imprisonment that lasted from AD 60 to 62. Upon his release, he left the city for a season of ministry. Peter would have arrived in Rome and written his first letter after Paul had left sometime in AD 62. Peter's second letter would have been written shortly after his first, close to the time of his death. At some point Paul returned to Rome, and tradition has it that Paul and Peter were both martyred in Rome in AD 64–65 under the persecution of Nero.[1]

Peter wrote "to the pilgrims of the Dispersion in Pontus, Galatia, Cappadocia, Asia, and Bithynia" (1:1). These believers had been scattered across regions in Asia Minor (places that were located in what is today Turkey). It is evident from Peter's letter that they were experiencing suffering. They were in need of Peter's exhortation and declaration of the true grace of God.

## The Purpose of 1 Peter

The overarching purpose of 1 Peter is stated clearly at the conclusion of the letter, "I have written to you briefly, exhorting and testifying that this is the true grace of God in which you stand" (5:12). As Peter declares the true grace of God and exhorts his readers to stand firm in it, he extinguishes the misconception that suffering for Christ's sake is strange. Contrarily, suffering is the way of the Savior, and since Christians follow in His footsteps, we are to expect suffering.

The purpose of 1 Peter becomes even clearer when we take a look at some key verses in his letter.

- He declares God's grace and peace to his readers (1:2; 5:12).
- He reminds us of our hope and exhorts us to be genuine in our faith, to the glory of God (1:3–7).

---

1. D. A. Carson and Douglas J. Moo, *An Introduction to the New Testament* (1992; repr., Grand Rapids: Zondervan, 2005), 643.

- He is careful to display the continuity between the Old and New Testament church (1:10–12).

- He teaches us that holiness is by the ordinary means of grace, which include the Word, sacraments, and prayer (1:13–2:3).

- He teaches us that true freedom is found in serving God and submitting to our authorities (2:16).

- He teaches us that suffering for righteousness' sake is a blessing (3:14).

- He defines the gospel as the life, death, resurrection, ascension, and second coming of Christ (3:18–22).

- He exhorts us to glorify God in all our words and works (4:11).

- He teaches us that servant leadership is the way of the Shepherd Leader (5:1–5).

- He teaches us that a firm faith grounds us when we are assaulted by the Enemy (5:8).

**An Outline of 1 Peter**

Different and more detailed outlines of 1 Peter can be found in commentaries, but for this Bible study, I suggest the following:

I. Living as Saints (1:1–2:10)

II. Living as Strangers (2:11–4:11)

III. Living as Sufferers (4:12–5:14)

Each lesson will further divide this broad outline into smaller parts, but for now note these major divisions as you prepare to study 1 Peter.

Perhaps you are grappling with questions like these: Who am I? How do I find peace? Is there any hope? If God cares about me, why am I suffering? Or maybe you are not sure how to define the true grace of God. I hope and pray that you will find the answers to your questions as you study Peter's declaration of the true grace of God.

# Our Home, Our Hope, Our Holiness

1 Peter 1:1–2:3

## Purpose . . .

**Head.** What do I need to know from this passage in Scripture?

- The same God who has chosen me out of His love and grace also secures my home, my hope, and my holiness.

**Heart.** How does what I learn from this passage affect my internal relationship with the Lord?

- I am a kingdom disciple who rejoices in my salvation and reveals a genuine faith in the midst of trials.

**Hands.** How does what I learn from this passage translate into action for God's kingdom?

- I will help others set their hope fully on Christ.
- I will exhort others to holiness.
- I will help others learn God's word.
- I will pray that the Lord would save my non-Christian family, friends, and neighbors.

## Personal Study . . .

**Pray.** Ask that God will open up your heart and mind as you study His Word. This is His story of redemption that He has revealed to us, and the Holy Spirit is our teacher.

**Ponder the Passage.** Read 1 Peter in its entirety. Then reread 1 Peter 1:1–2:3.

- *Point.* What is the point of this passage? How does this relate to the point of the entire book?

- *People.* Who are the main people involved in this passage? What characterizes them?

- *Persons of the Trinity.* Where do you see God the Father, God the Son, and God the Holy Spirit in this passage?

- *Puzzling Parts.* Are there any parts of the passage that you don't quite understand or that seem interesting or confusing?

**Put It in Perspective.**

- *Place in Scripture.* What is the original context of this text? What is the redemptive-historical context—what has or hasn't happened in redemptive history at this point in Scripture? How does this text connect to Christ?

*The following questions will help if you got stuck on any of the previous questions, and they will help you dig a little deeper into the text, putting it all into perspective.*

1. **1:1–2.** (a) The Gospels and the book of Acts give us a lot of background on the apostle Peter that is helpful to know as we read 1 Peter. Using a concordance or another Bible tool, what do you learn about Peter from these books?

(b) To whom is Peter writing? How does what he calls his readers ("pilgrims," or in some Bible translations, "exiles") make them identify with Old Testament Israel, which was taken into captivity by the Assyrians and Babylonians?

(c) According to these verses, why does Peter call them "pilgrims," or in some Bible translations, "exiles"?

(d) How are all three persons of the Godhead involved in our salvation?

(e) Read Exodus 24:3–8. What is happening in this passage? Which part of 1:2 references this passage?

(f) Using Scripture, how would you define God's grace and peace?

**2.** (a) How did Jesus experience exile for our salvation?

(b) Like Peter's readers, the church today lives in the world as pilgrims. How does looking back toward Jesus's life, death, resurrection, and ascension, as well as looking forward to His return, help us endure as pilgrims?

**3. 1:3–5.** (a) What does it mean to bless God (for example, see Ps. 34:1)? Why can we bless God (see Num. 6:24–27)?

(b) What attribute of God does our salvation reveal?

(c) To what are we born again?

(d) What is the foundation of our hope?

(e) What is being reserved in heaven for us?

(f) How does the description of our inheritance contrast with the promised land Old Testament Israel received (see Isa. 24:3–4; 40:8; Jer. 2:7)?

(g) By what and through what are we being kept?

(h) According to Scripture, what is faith (see Heb. 11:1)?

(i) For what are we being kept?

(j) How has our salvation already been revealed on the one hand, and not yet on the other?

**4. 1:6–9.** (a) In what do we rejoice?

(b) How do trials test the genuineness of our faith?

(c) What will result in praise, honor, and glory at the revelation of Christ?

(d) How are we to respond to Jesus, even though we have not seen Him?

(e) What is the end of our faith?

**5. 1:10–12.** (a) About what did the prophets prophesy, search, and inquire carefully?

(b) Who was at work in them, indicating the prophecies they gave?

(c) How did they know they were serving future believers, not themselves, when they prophesied?

(d) Who was at work in those who preached the gospel to Peter's readers?

(e) Into what things do angels desire to look?

(f) Compare this passage with Luke 24:25–27, 44–49. What do you learn from your comparison?

**6. 1:13.** (a) In verse 13, "therefore" is an important word because it shows that Peter is going to be building on ideas he has previously mentioned. What are these ideas?

(b) What does Peter call his readers to do?

(c) How does he tell them to do this?

(d) Read Exodus 12:11. What is the context of that verse? How does "gird up the loins of your mind" allude to it?

(e) Peter tells his readers to "be sober," rather than being drunk. How would drunkenness hinder them from fully setting their hope on the grace promised at Christ's revelation?

**7. 1:14–16.** (a) What is and is not to characterize our relationship with our heavenly Father?

(b) Look up Leviticus 11:44 (see also Lev. 11:45; 19:2; 20:7). How does Peter reference these passages here?

(c) What does it mean to be holy?

**8. 1:17–21.** (a) Peter emphasizes that God is our Father and judge. What else is He to us (see v. 18)? How are we to respond to Him as such (see also Ps. 34:11)?

(b) What are some examples of "aimless conduct" Peter's readers inherited from their forefathers? Contrast your examples with the Lord's ways (see Ps. 34:22).

(c) How are "corruptible things" different from the "precious blood of Christ"?

(d) Read Exodus 12. What is happening in that chapter? What language does Peter use in verse 19 that references Exodus 12?

(e) From what time was Christ foreordained?

(f) When was He made manifest, and for whose sake was He made manifest?

(g) What two things did God do for His Son?

(h) In what are the believer's faith and hope to rest?

**9. 1:22–2:3.** (a) How does embracing the truth of the gospel enable us to love our brothers and sisters in Christ?

(b) How does Peter use the imagery of procreation to contrast how we are born naturally with how we are born into God's family? What role does the word of God serve in this?

(c) What is the contrast depicted in Isaiah 40:6, 8, and what is Peter emphasizing by using it?

(d) Of what does the word consist?

(e) To what does the "therefore" of 2:1 refer, and why is it important in light of Peter's imperatives (what we are to do)?

(f) How does Peter use the imagery of a newborn infant to urge his readers to grow in salvation?

(g) Using your cross references, find out which psalm Peter is alluding to in 2:3.

**Principles and Points of Application**

**10. 1:1–2.** (a) How does Peter's testimony (an unconverted fisherman in Galilee to an apostle of Jesus Christ) encourage you?

(b) In what ways are you experiencing exile right now?

(c) In the midst of your exile, consider that Christ endured exile from heaven to save sinners like you and me. How does that encourage you?

**11. 1:3–12.** (a) Use 1:3–9 as a guide to write out a prayer of praise to the Lord.

(b) What have you learned about the continuity between the Old Testament and the New Testament in this passage? How has 1:10–12 encouraged you to see Christ in all of Scripture?

**12. 1:13–2:3.** (a) How will you set your hope fully on Christ this week? (Be specific as you think through how you will prepare your mind for action and how you will be sober-minded.)

(b) Living a holy life sounds daunting, but we must remember that we are children of the Holy One and He is conforming us to Christ's image. His power enables us to live in holiness (see 2 Peter 1:3). What areas of your life need to be brought into conformity with God's holiness?

(c) If you are a true believer, spend time in prayer today, thanking the Lord for redeeming you.

**13. 1:22–2:3.** (a) How does God's Word both inform and transform your love for your brothers and sisters in Christ?

(b) How often do you ingest God's Word (see Ps. 119:103)?

(c) With whom do you need to share the gospel this week?

(d) What malice, deceit, hypocrisy, envy, and slander do you need to repent of today?

(e) How have you tasted that the Lord is good in your study of Scripture?

(f) How will you prioritize Bible study, recognizing that you cannot know the Lord apart from His Word?

(g) How will you teach those under your leadership to do the same?

## Putting It All Together...

After forty-nine showings to sell our old home and living for five months in an apartment, we were excited to finally move into our newly built house. The reason for our move was to be closer to our church family, and we thought we had chosen a great location. But after we moved in, I learned that facts about our family had been misconstrued before we arrived, leading people to believe all kinds of interesting things about us. After our arrival it became obvious that we did not fit into the established friendships and lifestyles around us. Rather than having backyard barbecues to share the gospel with my neighbors, I found myself tempted to retreat into the walls of my house. I felt like an exile on my own street, unwelcomed by those around me.

I shouldn't have been as surprised as I was that all my neighbors didn't welcome me with open arms. Ultimately, they weren't rejecting me, but Jesus, whom I professed to be Lord. Though long, the trial ingrained a truth in my heart that I had been slow to learn. The very faith that saves us is also the faith that sets us apart from the world and often invites others' dislike. Jesus showed us that the way to glory is through suffering. We must fix our eyes on Him, the builder of our heavenly home.

Peter reminds us in his letter that this world is not our home, our hope is not in earthly treasure, and our holiness is to reflect our heavenly Father. Trials often serve to remind us of these truths. Feeling like a stranger on my own street nailed me to my knees, riveted my eyes to my Redeemer, and drove me to delight in His Word, not the world around me.

## I. Living as Saints: Our Home (1:1–2)

One of the first things I do before I read a book is identify the author. Knowing the author helps me understand the worldview that informs his or her writing, which is important. When we come to 1 Peter, the information on the author is scant: "Peter, an apostle of Jesus Christ" (1:1), yet in that one phrase we immediately recognize that Peter's writing will be informed by Christ. Indeed, the Spirit of Christ wrote through Peter (2 Peter 1:20–21). There is much more we can learn about Peter from the Gospels and the book of Acts, though. It would be wise for us to turn our attention to his background before we read his letter. It will inform and illuminate his letter and bring us to a deeper appreciation of what he says and why he says it.

Peter, an ordinary man from Bethsaida, a city in Galilee, knew what it was to be transformed by grace, receiving a new name. Instead of calling him Simon, Jesus changed his name to Cephas, which means "Peter," from the word *rock*. The trade he knew and loved so well as a fisherman on the Sea of Galilee paled in comparison to the trade he learned when Christ made him a fisher of men and to the love and grace he experienced when Jesus saved him. He was called by Christ to be a kingdom worshiper, appointed by Christ to be a kingdom worker, and sent out by Christ to be a kingdom witness (Mark 3:16).

Because Peter was called as one of God's children, he was able to confess Jesus as the Christ (Mark 8:29). He knew that Jesus alone had the words of eternal life (John 6:68) and was the Holy One of God. He had witnessed the miraculous power of God when Jesus raised Jairus's daughter from death to life (Mark 5:35–43) and healed his mother-in-law's fever (Matt. 8:14–15). He also knew the mighty power of God when he witnessed that Jesus walked on the water and then enabled him to walk on the water as well—until he doubted, that is. But even when Peter doubted, Jesus graciously reached out His hand to save him from sinking, displaying His grace and love to him (Matt. 14:28–29).

Peter had watched as Jesus was transfigured before him on the mountain and had been overwhelmed with terror by the event. When he suggested making three tents, one each for Jesus, Moses, and Elijah, he learned a lesson concerning Christ's pre-eminence. The Father will not give His glory to anyone other than His Son. He also learned that day that Jesus would rise from the dead, but he had no idea what that meant (Mark 9:2–13).

Peter was also acquainted with the truth that in God's kingdom, the first will be last and the last will be first (Matt. 19:30; 20:16; Mark 10:31; Luke 13:30). Peter had heard Jesus curse a fig tree and had seen it wither, learning a lesson in faith, prayer, and forgiveness (Mark 11:21). He had privately sat on the Mount of Olives with Jesus, along with James, John, and Andrew, and had received a lesson on the signs of the end of the age (Mark 13:3–37). And he had eaten the last Passover with Jesus before His death (Mark 14:12–25).

Peter had learned many lessons in humility as well. When he confidently asserted before Jesus that he would never fall way from Him, Jesus corrected him by foretelling his three denials. Peter confirmed his need for correction not only when he denied Jesus three times but also when he fell asleep in the garden of Gethsemane when he was supposed to be praying (Mark 14:29–72). On the occasion when Jesus stooped to wash Peter's feet, he wanted no part in it until Jesus informed him he would have no part with Him if he refused. Then Peter wanted Jesus to wash his hands and head as well (John 13:6–37). When he tried to defend Jesus with the sword, cutting off Malchus's ear, he was reprimanded by Jesus, in whose kingdom suffering, not the sword, is the weapon to wield (John 18:10–27).

How gracious it was that the Lord would have Peter, in light of all his failures, be one of the first to see the empty tomb and the first of the Twelve to behold the Savior (John 20:2–6; 1 Cor. 15:5). He was also privileged to privately hear the gracious, forgiving voice of his Master asking three times if he loved Him (to match Peter's three denials) and instructing him to feed His sheep and follow Him. At the same time, he learned that following Christ would end in a martyr's death (John 21:15–19). Peter's failures would have disqualified him for the ministry except for the forgiving grace of God. He also received the greatest class in teaching Christ in all of Scripture when Jesus opened the disciples' minds to understand everything written about Him in the Old Testament (Luke 24:44–48). As Paul so beautifully reminds us, "All the promises of God in Him are Yes" (2 Cor. 1:20).

Peter was not only impacted by Jesus's life, death, and resurrection but also deeply influenced by His ascension, the day of Pentecost, and the beginning days of the New Testament church (Acts 1:6–20). Peter put the preaching lesson given by Jesus into practice on the day of Pentecost, proclaiming a redemptive-historical message to his listeners (Acts 2:14–38). His days were busy with teaching about the kingdom of God and performing signs and wonders that pointed to God's power and saving grace (Acts 3:1–12; 9:32–43). He knew what it was to suffer in prison for the sake of Jesus and at the same time God's miraculous power to release him (Acts 4:1–23; 5:17–42; 12:3–18). He boldly confronted the sin of Ananias and Sapphira as well as Simon the magician (Acts 5:1–11; 8:9–24). Peter went with John to Samaria when they heard the Samaritans had received the word of God and prayed that they would receive the Holy Spirit also (Acts 8:14–17). After Peter received a vision that Jesus had made all foods clean and learned that God shows no partiality between Jews and Gentiles, the Holy Spirit fell on the Gentiles while he preached to them in Cornelius's home (Acts 10:5–48). Peter told the Jerusalem church of the Gentile conversion, acknowledging he had been appointed by God to share the gospel with Gentiles so that they might believe and be saved (Acts 15:7).

Peter also knew the apostle Paul. Paul visited Peter in Jerusalem and stayed with him for fifteen days (Gal. 1:18). Paul tells us that Peter had been entrusted with the gospel to the Jews and that he was a pillar (along with John and James, the Lord's brother) of the Jerusalem church (Gal. 2:7–9). Peter extended fellowship to Paul, blessing his calling to the Gentiles and asking him to remember the poor as he ministered (Gal. 2:8–10). Paul also exposed one of Peter's weaknesses when he opposed his hypocrisy of eating with Gentiles when the circumcision party wasn't around, but not eating with Gentiles when they were. This revealed Peter's fear of man, and Paul corrected him, reminding him that the Lord had made all foods clean (Gal. 2:11–14), a lesson Peter had previously learned (Acts 10:9–33).

As important as it is to know about Peter, we also need to know about his original readers. As we learn about Peter's readers and their home, we also learn about our home. Like Peter's original readers who were pilgrims (some Bible translations say "exiles") of God living in dispersed places, we are pilgrims of God living in a place that is not our true home. Peter pulls his language from the Old Testament, alluding to the exile of the Jews at the hands of the Assyrians and the Babylonians.[1] The reason for Israel's exile was judgment, but the reason for the readers' exile was grace. Christ's first coming had inaugurated the kingdom of God, and they were living as pilgrims, knowing their inheritance of their heavenly home was already in place for them. They may have been exiled and scattered across regions in Asia Minor (places that were located in what is today Turkey), but they were elect, God's chosen children. Their scattering was sure to end in God's sweeping finale of salvation history, Christ's second coming, which will bring judgment on those who refused to bow their knee to Christ on this earth and salvation for all who believed in His name. Christ will usher all of God's children to their heavenly home.

---

1. The term *Dispersion* referred to the Jews who had been scattered throughout the world following the Babylonian exile that happened in three deportations (605, 597, and 586 BC). Initially the scattering was forced, but over time Jews chose to emigrate. Edmund Clowney, *The Message of 1 Peter* (Downers Grove, Ill.: InterVarsity, 1988), 37.

Not only was their past certain (they had been chosen by the foreknowledge of God the Father, their salvation applied by the sanctifying work of the Holy Spirit, and their redemption bought by the precious blood of Jesus) and their future secure (He had chosen them to be His for all eternity), their present was filled with grace and peace. God's foreknowledge has nothing to do with whether we've been naughty or nice; it has everything to do with God's gracious lovingkindness. The Spirit sanctifies us, bringing us from death to new life at our initial conversion, and then progressively working in our lives to conform us more and more to the image of Christ, a process that won't be perfected until glory. Jesus has lived a life of perfect obedience on our behalf, and now the Spirit enables us to live in obedience as children of our Father. Christ has sprinkled us with His blood, atoning for our sins, so that we might be reconciled to God. All three persons of the Godhead are intricately involved in our salvation, a truth that should lead us to a life of praise for God's glorious grace.

Peter alludes to the covenant God made with Old Testament Israel when he speaks of the sprinkling of Jesus's blood (Ex. 24:3–8). After the Lord had delivered Israel from Egypt and brought them safely to the foot of Mount Sinai, the people entered into a covenant with Him to obey all His commands. The Lord had saved them and brought them to Himself, but they had to keep His covenant in order to be a kingdom of priests and a holy nation. Throughout the history of redemption, we learn that Israel failed to do this. It was only the true Israel, Jesus Christ, who fulfilled the law perfectly as the greatest and final priest and Holy One of Israel, and enables God's people to be holy as well (2 Peter 1:3–5). Because we are in covenant with God and with one another, our lives that may appear to be wracked with gruesome trials and petrifying suffering are instead wrapped in the grace and peace of our great God, who has loved us and redeemed us as His own and is keeping us safe until He takes us to our true home.

## II. Living as Saints: Our Hope (1:3–12)

Peter bursts forth with blessing, praising the God who has blessed him. He knows God as Father because he knows Jesus Christ as Lord. God the Father, in His mercy, has caused believers to be born again to a living hope, which is founded on the resurrection of Jesus Christ from the dead. We do not hope in the worldly sense, wishing that we'll get lucky and some large fortune will come to us. We hope in God. Our hope is certain because Jesus's resurrection is already a fact in history that has been accomplished. His resurrection in the past secures our inheritance in the future, an inheritance that is kept safe for us in heaven. Unlike the promised land of Canaan, which perished, became defiled by Israel's sin, and faded before Israel's eyes while the people were carried off into exile (see 2 Kings 24:10–25:21), our heavenly inheritance will never grow corrupt, will never become defiled, and will never fade. It is eternal and pure, inhabited by glorified saints and filled with the immeasurable glory of God and Christ. Peter's words echo Christ's as He preached the Sermon on the Mount, "Do not lay up for yourselves treasures on earth, where moth and rust destroy and where thieves break in and steal; but lay up for yourselves treasures in heaven, where neither moth nor rust destroys and where thieves do not break in and steal. For where your treasure is, there your heart will be also" (Matt. 6:19–21).

God's power is guarding believers through faith for a coming salvation that has already been inaugurated. Such a salvation is cause for rejoicing, regardless of wretched circumstances that swirl around us and threaten to undo us at every point. Such trials test our faith, revealing whether it is genuine. Genuine faith is lasting faith. Unlike gold that ultimately perishes even though it is refined by fire to remove impurities, saving faith results in eternal life with Jesus Christ our Lord, to whom all praise, glory, and honor is due. Our entire lives should be lived for His glory, including the grievous parts. Our suffering is not in vain; it showcases our Savior, who suffered first on our behalf.

Peter had seen Jesus and loved Him, believed in Him, and rejoiced with inexpressible and glorious joy in the faith that he had received. He must have been encouraged that his readers, who had not yet seen Jesus, also loved Him and believed in Him. When Thomas refused to believe the disciples' report of the resurrection, Jesus appeared to him, letting him place his finger on His hands and side and imploring him to believe, which Thomas did. Jesus replied to him, "Thomas, because you have seen Me, you have believed. Blessed are those who have not seen and yet have believed" (John 20:29).

Peter's readers not only loved Jesus and believed in Him but also rejoiced with inexpressible and glorious joy in the faith they had received. One reason the salvation of our souls is cause for rejoicing is because it is the fulfillment of redemptive history. All through the Old Testament, the prophets proclaimed the coming Christ. The Spirit of Christ was in them, indicating His own sufferings and glories to come. The Christ who is the fulfillment of Scripture is also the Christ who is the author of Scripture. As Scripture moved forward toward the climax of His life, death, and resurrection, His Spirit moved men's pens to record redemptive history. It was even revealed to the prophets that they were serving future generations of believers as they wrote of things that pointed forward to the good news of Christ. The Holy Spirit continued to work in the lives of the apostles as they taught the gospel in the days of the early church, proclaiming the kingdom of God and teaching about the Lord and Savior Jesus Christ, truths that are so glorious even the angels long to look into them.

Jesus told His disciples, "Blessed are your eyes for they see, and your ears for they hear; for assuredly, I say to you that many prophets and righteous men desired to see what you see, and did not see it, and to hear what you hear, and did not hear it" (Matt. 13:16–17). Peter stressed to his suffering readers that they were privileged people indeed. They were living on this side of the cross and had the privilege of hearing the apostle's teaching, which continues to proclaim the kingdom of God and teach about the life, death, resurrection, ascension, and second coming of Christ through the written Word of God.

Perhaps you feel void of hope today. Take heart in the word of the living God that reminds you of the hope you have, which is founded on the resurrection of our Lord and Savior Jesus Christ. He has mercifully given us new life in Christ, is keeping our inheritance for us, and is guarding us by His power. Our hearts, no matter what our circumstances, should rejoice in who He is, what He has done, what He is doing, and what He will do. Our hands, no matter our trials, should be raised to Him in adoration and praise. Our eyes, no matter our weakness, should be fixed on His glory. And our feet, no matter our fears, should be steadfast on His path. We have something far better than good days ahead of us. We have the inheritance of the Lord Jesus Christ Himself, who loves us and gave Himself for us.

### III. Living as Saints: Our Holiness (1:13–2:3)

The hope of the gospel reminds us that our heavenly home is secure, our temporary trials are purposeful, and our holiness is the right response. God's grace saves us for a life of holiness, not licentiousness. His power has provided what we need for holy living (2 Peter 1:3–5); we don't conjure it up by our own strength and willpower. Setting our hope fully on the coming grace that has already been inaugurated is work, but it is work done in the power of God's Spirit working in us.

To fully set our hope on grace, we must gird up the loins of our mind, an allusion to how Israel ate the first Passover as they prepared to leave Egypt in a hurry (Ex. 12:11) and possibly to Jesus's words in the parable about being ready for His second coming (Luke 12:35–36). Our minds will be assaulted with all kinds of temptations to take our hope off the grace of Jesus Christ, so we must be prepared to fight such temptations with truth. We must also be sober-minded. Drunkenness dulls our senses and prohibits us from setting our hope fully on God's grace. When we are drunk, our hope is usually set on something else. We hope the drink will drown our despair, but it does the opposite—it drowns us in despair.

Peter reminded his readers that they were children of obedience; they have a perfect heavenly Father and a Savior who obeyed the law on their behalf. Therefore, they were not to live as children of disobedience with the Father of Lies and the false saviors of the flesh they formerly knew before they were converted. Instead, they were to be holy because the One who called them to Himself is holy. The imperative (what we are to do) is grounded in the indicative (what God has already done for us). Peter quoted from Leviticus 19:2, a powerful reminder that although the ceremonial law is no longer binding on God's people, the moral law continues to teach us many things.[2] It has not been displaced, but fulfilled by Jesus Christ, and now gives us a track on which to

---

2. It informs us of God's holy nature and will, convinces us of our inability to keep it, humbles us in our sense of sin, helps us to see our desperate need of Christ and His perfect obedience, shows us how much we are bound to Christ for His fulfilling it and enduring the curse of God in our place, provokes us to more thankfulness, and helps us conform to it as the rule of our obedience. See the Westminster Larger Catechism, answers 95 and 97.

run the race of grace. Holiness is not possible apart from Christ to be sure, but it is certainly possible with Christ. Grace transforms us from the inside out, changing our lives to reflect Jesus, though not perfectly on this side of glory.

Peter had learned that his heavenly Father judges impartially according to each one's deeds (Acts 10:34). All those who are His children are to conduct themselves accordingly. Reverent fear before the Redeemer is the right response during our pilgrimage on this earth—not casual conduct before the Creator. Peter's readers had been ransomed by Jesus Christ, who bought them back from slavery to sin and freed them to new life.

The Gentiles to whom Peter was writing had been steeped in futile ways from their forefathers, seeking precious metals of this world. Since they had been sought by God and bought by Christ's blood, Peter told them that they were to live a different way. Jesus is the way, the truth, and the life (John 14:6) and has always been the way since before the foundation of the world. He was the Lamb of which all the sacrificial lambs of the Old Testament were only shadows. God had required Old Testament Israel to bring unblemished lambs to the tabernacle and temple for sacrifice because they were types of Him who was to come, the perfect One. Peter's readers, living in the last times (just as we are), had the privilege of looking back toward the resurrection and forward to His second coming, knowing their faith and hope were secure in the God who raised Jesus from the dead and who will send Him again to save those eagerly waiting for Him.

Peter points his readers to the truth. Immersing ourselves in the truth, the Word of God, is a means of grace God uses to purify our souls, leading to a right relationship with Him, but also to a right relationship with others. We can love our brothers and sisters earnestly only from a pure heart. At salvation we receive a new heart (not a perfect heart), and the Spirit who writes God's word upon our hearts also enables us to obey it (Jer. 31:33; 2 Peter 1:3–5). Peter's exhortation to love one another earnestly is rooted in the concept of covenant. When we enter into a covenant relationship with the Lord, we become part of the family of God. No longer lone rangers, we are placed in the community of faith. Isolationism and individualism must be abandoned and the covenant community embraced. Just as the Father, Son, and Holy Spirit retain their distinctions within the Godhead, so too we retain our individual callings and gifts in the midst of unity and community.

Peter compares our new birth with our physical birth. We have been born again of seed, but it is seed that is imperishable, like our inheritance (1:4). We have been born again through the living and abiding word of God. Peter quotes Isaiah 40:6–8 to contrast the glory of mankind with the glory of God. Our physical birth that brings us into life on this earth begins to perish and fade the moment we are born. In contrast, the word of God remains forever—glorious, steady, strong, and sure. This word of God is nothing less than the gospel, which unfolds on the pages of both the Old and New Testaments. We must study the whole word of God, Genesis through Revelation, teaching Christ in all of Scripture.

Since we have received the good news by faith and have been born again to a living hope through the resurrection of Jesus Christ, we are to put away those things that characterized our old life. Malice, deceit, hypocrisy, envy, and slander are not to characterize Christians. We have been freed from sin in order to live holy lives by the power of the Spirit who sanctifies. Peter has already compared our new life in Christ with the beginning of our physical life. We have been born again through the imperishable seed of the word of God, and it is this same word that will continually nourish our souls. Peter exhorts his readers to long for the pure spiritual milk, which is the key to their growth in salvation.

If you've ever been around a nursing newborn, you know what longing Peter is talking about. Newborns don't settle for milk substitutes easily, and they cry loudly for such sustenance. Likewise, believers shouldn't settle for milk substitutes, even good ones like devotionals and Christian literature. Reading Christian books isn't harmful until they become a substitute for the Bible. Our hearts should cry loudly to be fed the word of God. Once we have tasted that the Lord, the living Word who reveals Himself in the written Word, is good, we will hunger for more and more of the word. Peter again alludes to Psalm 34, this time to verse 8: "Oh, taste and see that the LORD is good; blessed is the man who trusts in Him!" Christians should love their Bibles and read and study them often. Like John Bunyan, the Puritan and author of *Pilgrim's Progress*, we should bleed the Bible when we are pricked.

Bunyan had tasted that the Lord is good, and he kept going back for more. I pray that you and I would do the same. It is time for us to stop saying we are too busy to read the Bible. Indeed, we are too busy *not* to read it. In it Christ reveals Himself to us. Apart from it we make saviors of our own liking. Such saviors prove to be false, futile, and fleeting in the end. But the word of God lasts forever. We should feed upon it as often as we satisfy our hunger and thirst with food and water, crying out with the psalmist, "How sweet are Your words to my taste, sweeter than honey to my mouth!" (Ps. 119:103).

Perhaps you can relate to my new-neighborhood experience, or maybe today you have lost all hope, or perhaps you are living in licentiousness with holiness far from your mind. Whatever the case, I hope you have been encouraged by Peter's words this week. Our heavenly home is secure. Our hope is certain. And our holiness is being worked out by the power of the Holy Spirit.

# *Processing It Together...*

1. What do we learn about God in 1 Peter 1:1–2:3?

2. How does this reshape how we should view our present circumstances?

3. What do we learn about God's Son, Jesus Christ?

4. How should this impact our relationship with God and with others?

5. What do we learn about God's covenant with His people?

6. How are we to live in light of this?

7. How can we apply 1 Peter 1:1–2:3 to our lives today and in the future?

8. How should we apply these verses in our churches?

9. Looking back at "Put It in Perspective" in your personal study questions, what did you find challenging or encouraging about this lesson?

10. Looking back at "Principles and Points of Application," how has this lesson impacted your life?

# A Spiritual House, a Special Honor, and a Significant Heritage

1 Peter 2:4–10

*Purpose*...

**Head.** What do I need to know from this passage in Scripture?

- Christ is the cornerstone upon which my significant heritage in the past, my being built into a spiritual house in the present, and my special honor in the future rests.

**Heart.** How does what I learn from this passage affect my internal relationship with the Lord?

- I am a kingdom disciple who recognizes who I am—a member of a chosen race, a royal priesthood, a holy nation, and a people for God's own possession.

**Hands.** How does what I learn from this passage translate into action for God's kingdom?

- I will offer spiritual sacrifices acceptable to God through Jesus Christ.
- I will exercise my spiritual gifts for the building of the spiritual house (the church).
- I will endure trials with my eyes fixed on the hope of my future honor with Christ.
- I will pray for those I know who are in need of salvation and take the opportunity to share the gospel with them.
- I will proclaim the excellencies of Him who called me out of darkness into His marvelous light.

# Personal Study...

**Pray.** Ask that God will open up your heart and mind as you study His Word. This is His story of redemption that He has revealed to us, and the Holy Spirit is our teacher.

**Ponder the Passage.** Read 1 Peter 2:4–10.

- *Point.* What is the point of this passage? How does this relate to the point of the entire book?
- *People.* Who are the main people involved in this passage? What characterizes them?
- *Persons of the Trinity.* Where do you see God the Father, God the Son, and God the Holy Spirit in this passage?
- *Puzzling Parts.* Are there any parts of the passage that you don't quite understand or that seem interesting or confusing?

**Put It in Perspective.**

- *Place in Scripture.* Since you have studied 1 Peter's place in Scripture in lesson 1, you may want to take this opportunity to review your answer.

*The following questions will help if you got stuck on any of the previous questions, and they will help you dig a little deeper into the text, putting it all into perspective.*

**1. 2:4.** (a) To whom do we come?

(b) How does the beginning of this verse reflect Psalm 34:4–5, 11?

(c) Read Acts 4:11–12. What similarities do you see between the imagery Peter uses as he addresses the Jewish council, and the imagery he uses in this verse?

(d) Who else uses this imagery, and to whom is He referring when He uses it (see Matt. 21:42–44; Mark 12:10–11; Luke 20:17–18)?

(e) Check your cross-references to find at least three different passages in the Old Testament that use this stone imagery. To whom are these Old Testament passages referring, and what does this tell you about Scripture as a whole?

(f) Contrast the welcome Jesus receives from men with the welcome He receives from His Father.

(g) How does this same contrast apply to Christians?

**2. 2:5.** (a) What imagery does Peter use to describe God's people?

(b) How does this imagery reflect both our individuality and community?

(c) Who is building us into a spiritual house?

(d) What two specific reasons does Peter mention for such a building project?

(e) Look up Exodus 19:5–6. How is Peter referring to that passage in this verse?

(f) What are some spiritual sacrifices Scripture mentions that are acceptable to God through Jesus Christ (for example, see Heb. 13:15–16)?

**3. 2:6.** (a) Read Isaiah 28:14–29, noting especially verse 16, which Peter cites in this verse.

(b) What is Peter explaining to his readers when he quotes this verse from Isaiah in his letter?

(c) Who is the fulfillment of this Scripture?

(d) Using a dictionary, define *cornerstone.* How is this an appropriate word for this context?

(e) What is the promise made to those who trust in Christ?

(f) How would this promise have encouraged Peter's readers?

**4. 2:7–8.** (a) What is Christ to believers?

(b) What do unbelievers fail to believe?

(c) Read Psalm 118:22 and Isaiah 8:13–14. Why does Peter reference these verses in his letter?

(d) Why do unbelievers stumble?

**5. 2:9.** (a) What phrases does Peter use to describe believers?

(b) For what purpose has God chosen us?

(c) What images does Peter use here to convey man's sin and God's holiness?

(d) Check your cross-references to see which Old Testament passages Peter is referring to in this verse. What was the context of those Old Testament passages? When Peter references these verses here, how is he continuing the theme that he began with his address to his readers in 1 Peter 1:1?

**6. 2:10.** (a) Contrast what believers once were with what they are now.

(b) Check your cross-references to see which Old Testament passage Peter is referring to in this verse.

(c) How has Christ made it possible for us to be reconciled to God and to receive mercy?

**Principles and Points of Application**

**7. 2:4.** (a) Have you ever come to Christ, confessing Him as Lord and Savior of your life?

(b) How does it encourage you in your present circumstances that Christ is chosen and precious in the sight of God, even though men reject Him?

**8. 2:5.** (a) How does Christ confirm our individuality and constitute a new community at the same time?

(b) Write down some of the encouragements and challenges you have experienced from being placed in a community of believers. What are some of the encouragements you experience from knowing that even though you are part of a community, you have been given individual gifts for the building up of the body of Christ and to glorify God?

(c) How are you involved in your local church, using your gifts for God's glory?

(d) How does your life reflect God's holiness?

(e) What are some of the spiritual sacrifices you are offering up to the Lord (see Heb. 13:15–16)?

**9. 2:6.** (a) In the midst of your present circumstances, how does the promise of this verse encourage you?

(b) Who is the cornerstone upon which you are being built? How does this encourage you?

**10. 2:7–8.** (a) Think of those you know who don't believe in Jesus Christ as Lord and Savior, or those who profess to believe in Him but have lifestyles that don't reflect their profession. Spend time in prayer for them today, asking the Lord to save them.

(b) Thank the Lord today for your salvation. He was the one who opened up your blind eyes, unstopped your deaf ears, and softened your hard heart. Praise Him!

**11. 2:9.** Who does Peter say that you are in Christ? How does the knowledge of who you already are in Christ lead you to a desire to proclaim the praises of God, who saved you from death and darkness to life and light?

**12. 2:10.** (a) As God's people who have received God's mercy, we should be quick to thank Him for such love by living lives of holiness, even under the heat of trials. Yet we often fall far short of a grateful response. Spend time today in confession and repentance, asking the Lord to kindle your love for Him and obedience to Him so that your life might glorify Him in all you say and do.

(b) As those who have received mercy, we should also be quick to extend mercy to others. Yet we often judge others instead. Confess this to the Lord today, acknowledging that He alone is judge. Consider the circumstances and whether you need to ask the person you judged for their forgiveness.

## Putting It All Together...

I was so thankful to finally get the carpet out of the house and have hardwood floors installed. I am allergic to dust and dust mites, so getting rid of the carpet would give me physical relief. After listening to the banging of hammers and watching workmen go up and down my steps many times, I was called upstairs. The supervisor of the job looked perplexed. He had come across a problem and wasn't sure he could fix it. The floors were not level. He pointed out to me that the walls were not level either. The builders of our home had failed to do their job correctly, and, instead of fixing it, they did their best to cover it up. But sooner or later, a poorly built foundation will be revealed. For us, that day came when we ripped up the carpet and realized that what carpet and a carpet pad can hide, hardwood floors can't. My husband had to work many, many hours trying to level the floor correctly so that the installers could lay the hardwoods properly.

The tiny trial of my hardwood floors illustrates an important spiritual truth. If the foundation of our hearts is not straight and true, then the way of our lives will not be straight and true either. There have been many things I have tried to make cornerstones (or foundations) in my life. When I was younger, success in academics and sports was important to me. But this did not make things straight and true for me. On the one hand, if I succeeded I began to fear I might not succeed again. On the other hand, if I failed I was left flailing my arms in hopelessness.

Fitness and healthy eating were also important to me. But soon I began to worship thinness and landed in a pit of despair. Relationships were important to me. If things were going well, I did well, but as soon as problems entered, I was challenged to the core. Achievement in ministry was important to me, but if I made a mistake or seemed to be put on the shelf for a time, I was tempted to think I was worthless.

Placing all these other things as cornerstones in my life caused the walls of my life building and the level of the floors not to be straight and true. It is only when Christ, my cornerstone, is the foundation of my life that everything else is made right. Peter has much to teach us in this passage about Christ, our cornerstone.

## I. Living as Saints: A Spiritual House (2:4–5)

In the previous verse (2:3), Peter referred to Psalm 34:8, "Oh, taste and see that the LORD is good!" Now, he refers to that psalm again, but to different verses:

> I sought the LORD, and He heard me,
> And delivered me from all my fears.
> They looked to Him and were radiant,
> And their faces were not ashamed....
> Come, you children, listen to me;
> I will teach you the fear of the LORD.
> —Ps. 34:4–5, 11

Psalm 34 is a psalm of deliverance, so it was appropriate for Peter to quote it to his readers, who were living under persecution. Throughout his letter, he kept pointing them to their hope that was grounded in the past (Christ's resurrection), the present (the living Word continues to speak to them through the written Word), and the future (Jesus is coming again). We see those three aspects in this lesson as well. They are being built up as a spiritual house (the present), they have a significant heritage (the past), and they will receive a special honor (the future). One of Peter's great desires (and assumptions) is that his readers have tasted that the Lord is good through the word of God, because they have come to Christ. The Bible reveals Jesus. When we come to Scripture, we do not come to a dead book, but a living one. We come to the voice of the living God.

In the Old Testament, the Lord had spoken through the prophet Isaiah about a precious cornerstone in Zion that would be a blessing to those who believed but a stone of offense and a rock of stumbling to those who did not believe. Peter refers to these verses in Isaiah to confirm that Christ is the fulfillment of them. The context of Isaiah fits well with Peter's words to his readers:

> Do not say, "A conspiracy,"
> Concerning all that this people call a conspiracy,
> Nor be afraid of their threats, nor be troubled.
> The LORD of hosts, Him you shall hallow;
> Let Him be your fear,
> And let Him be your dread.
> *He will be as a sanctuary,*
> *But a stone of stumbling and a rock of offense*
> *To both the houses of Israel,*
> As a trap and a snare to the inhabitants of Jerusalem.
> *And many among them shall stumble;*
> *They shall fall and be broken,*
> *Be snared and taken.*
> (Isa. 8:12–15; italics highlight the verses Peter references)

Also,

> Therefore thus says the Lord GOD:
> "Behold, I lay in Zion a stone for a foundation,
> A tried stone, a precious cornerstone, a sure foundation;
> Whoever believes will not act hastily." (Isa. 28:16)

Peter refers to the psalmist's words as well:

> The stone which the builders rejected
> Has become the chief cornerstone.
> This was the LORD's doing;
> It is marvelous in our eyes. (Ps. 118:22–23)

When Jesus told the parable of the tenants, He quoted Psalm 118:22–23:

> Jesus said to them, "Have you never read in the Scriptures:
> 'The stone which the builders rejected
> Has become the chief cornerstone.
> This was the LORD's doing,
> And it is marvelous in our eyes'?

33

> "Therefore I say to you, the kingdom of God will be taken from you and given to a nation bearing the fruits of it. And whoever falls on this stone will be broken; but on whomever it falls, it will grind him to powder." (Matt. 21:42–44)

The chief priests and the Pharisees who heard Him speak this parable and perceived He was speaking about them would have arrested Him there and then, except they feared the people who thought that Jesus was a prophet (Matt. 21:45–46).

Addressing the Jewish council after Jesus's death, resurrection, and ascension and after the day of Pentecost, Peter used this same stone imagery in his defense before them:

> Then Peter, filled with the Holy Spirit, said to them, "Rulers of the people and elders of Israel: If we this day are judged for a good deed done to a helpless man, by what means he has been made well, let it be known to you all, and to all the people of Israel, that by the name of Jesus Christ of Nazareth, whom you crucified, whom God raised from the dead, by Him this man stands here before you whole. This is the 'stone which was rejected by you builders, which has become the chief cornerstone.' Nor is there salvation in any other, for there is no other name under heaven given among men by which we must be saved." (Acts 4:8–12)

Peter's readers would most certainly have been comforted in their circumstances by these words. They had come to Christ, the One who was chosen and precious to God, though rejected by men. Peter was reminding them by referring to the psalmist and the prophet Isaiah that this was God's plan from the beginning. They too were chosen and precious to God, though rejected by men. And this too was God's plan from the beginning. They should not think something strange was happening to them (1 Peter 4:12). They were following the way of Christ. Not only this, they were part of a building program that was both purifying and purposeful.

God has had a grand design for His people from the beginning. He placed His Son as the cornerstone of the spiritual house when He was raised from the dead. The cornerstone is the most important stone; it is the foundational stone. It is imperative that the cornerstone is square and true, because the angle of the walls and the level of the stone courses will be determined by it.[1] If the cornerstone isn't square and true, the rest of the building won't be square and true either. Amazingly, believers are part of God's spiritual house as well. We are like living stones built upon Christ, the cornerstone.

This building program is, first, purifying ("a holy priesthood"). This phrase references Exodus 19:6, the context of which is Israel at Mount Sinai about to receive the Ten Commandments. They had been delivered from Egypt, and the Lord had brought

---

1. Clowney, *Message of 1 Peter*, 84.

them to Himself to be a holy priesthood. The Holy Spirit who initially sanctified us at conversion (1 Peter 1:2) continues to sanctify us as we grow more and more in Christ-likeness until we are perfected at Christ's second coming.

Second, this building program is purposeful ("to offer up spiritual sacrifices acceptable to God through Jesus Christ"). We are to glorify God with our entire lives. Whether in word or in works, we are to recognize Christ as the cornerstone who is pre-eminent in all things. As we sing praises to the Lord with our lips, serve others with our hands, and share our resources with those in need, all glory is to go to God. These two purposes encompass our mission as worshipers, workers, and witnesses in our Father's world. Worship brings glory to God and is our greatest witness to others. Work honors the King as we serve within His kingdom. And witness is one of our primary tasks as we await the return of our King (Matt. 28:18–20).

## II. Living as Saints: A Special Honor (2:6–8)

In 2:4–5, Peter grounds his readers in the future (they will receive a special honor) as well as in the present (they are being built up as a spiritual house). As a spiritual house, founded on Christ the cornerstone, they have a special honor awaiting them on the final day of judgment. This was important for Peter's readers, who were suffering shame at the hands of persecutors. Those who walked according to the wisdom of the world, disobeying the word of God and remaining dead in their trespasses and sins, were relentless in heaping shame upon those who walked according to the wisdom of God, obeying His word and exalting Him. Peter refers to several Old Testament passages in these verses to confirm three things. First, Christ is the fulfillment of Isaiah's prophecy regarding the chosen and precious cornerstone God laid in Zion. Second, Christians are a fulfillment of Isaiah's prophecy that whoever believes in the precious cornerstone won't be put to shame. And third, nonbelievers are the fulfillment of Isaiah's prophecy that the stone was one of stumbling for those who disobeyed the word, as they were destined to do.

In Isaiah 28:14–29, God spoke words of judgment against Israel and Jerusalem through Isaiah. His people had taken refuge in lies and made a covenant with death. All kinds of injustice and unrighteousness filled the people's hearts and land. The Lord prophesied that He would make things right again by way of a precious corner-stone that He had laid in Zion. Anyone who took refuge in His chosen stone, instead of in lies, would not be put to shame (Isa. 28:16).

Peter demonstrates that Christ is the fulfillment of this prophecy (He is the cor-nerstone) as are believers (those who believe in Him who will not be put to shame). Contrary to what Peter's readers were tempted to think under persecution, they were the special ones who should feel no shame. Those who should be ashamed were the unbelievers walking according to disobedience. On the day of judgment, far from receiving honor, they would receive dishonor. Peter used two Old Testament quotes to confirm this truth.

First, he quoted from Psalm 118:22 to prove that the unbelieving builders rejected the foundation of Christ, building on another foundation instead—that of their own ways and wickedness. Second, he quoted from Isaiah 8:13–14 to remind his readers that Christ, the fulfillment of the stone, was also an offense to those walking in disobedience. Peter's readers should not be surprised, therefore, that those who disobeyed the word around them had stumbled over Christ. Except for the grace of God, all mankind would stumble over the Stone, for we were all destined to destruction because of Adam's transgression. Amazingly, God has chosen to save some of us out of His free love and grace so that we are no longer left in our trespasses and sins, but have been brought from death to new life. The stoniness of our hearts has been rolled away by the Stone. He has stood in our stead and suffered on our behalf, bearing the shame that we all deserve. Those of us who are now in Christ will never be put to shame, because He received the highest honor when He was raised from the dead and ascended into heaven, where He was exalted at His Father's right hand of glory. Every knee will bow and every tongue will confess that He is Lord, to the glory of God the Father, when He appears again. Those who are eagerly waiting for Him will be to the praise of His glorious grace, but those who never believed in Him as Lord and Savior will be to the praise of His glorious justice.

### III. Living as Saints: A Significant Heritage (2:9–10)

Not only are Peter's readers (and all believers) being built into a spiritual house in the present and looking forward to special honor in the future, but they are also rooted in the past with a significant heritage. The New Testament church was not a completely new beginning of believers who placed their faith in a new person named Jesus. The Old Testament church was connected to the New Testament church in a similar way that a seed is connected to the final tree. There has always been one people of God, chosen by His love, for His glory. Peter makes this abundantly clear in these verses when he uses Old Testament language that previously described the nation of Israel in order to describe the church. Prior to choosing Israel as a nation, God had chosen individuals (Adam, Noah, Abraham), and then an entire family (Jacob and his twelve sons) to be His own. His purpose in choosing Israel had nothing to do with their greatness (they weren't great at all!), but everything to do with His free love and His plan of redemption (Deut. 7:7–8). They were to be a light to the nations, showing those around them what it meant to worship God.

Tragically, Israel fell into deep and grievous sin, incurring the worst of curses—exile. First the Northern Kingdom went into exile by the hand of the Assyrians, and then the Southern Kingdom went into exile by the hand of the Babylonians. God's promises seemed to be threatened on every side. But, in God's mercy, He sent His people prophets (Jeremiah, Daniel, and Ezekiel) to remind them that the God who judges is also the God of grace. Exile would not be the final word. The true Israel, Jesus Christ, the light of the nations, would be exiled from heaven in order to usher in the new covenant and inaugurate a new kingdom, the kingdom of God.

Though the nation of Israel had failed to be a chosen generation, a royal priesthood, a holy nation, and God's own special people, the true Israel did not fail. Jesus was born as a Jew (the chosen race), He was the final royal priest who offered the sacrifice of Himself to make atonement for man's sin (a royal priesthood), He was holy in all His ways (a holy nation), and was God's chosen and beloved Son (a people for His own possession). Christ came as both the servant, fulfilling what Israel should have fulfilled (the law), and the Lord, extending grace and peace to those dead in their trespasses and sins. Paul reminds us that not all of national Israel was true Israel (see Romans 9–11). From the beginning, the Lord brought others into His chosen people (think of Rahab, Ruth, and Naaman). Only those within Israel who believed in God and looked forward in faith to the fulfillment of His promises were saved.

When Christ came and fulfilled all the promises of God, He reorganized God's people. Just as there had been twelve tribes of Israel, He chose twelve apostles. Just as Israel was to be a light to the nations, so too the church was to be a light to the nations. But it was not completely the same. Israel had been a theocratic nation, giving God's people a picture of Christ's coming kingdom. When Christ came there was no longer any need for the theocratic nation of Israel. God's kingdom encompasses a people from every tribe, tongue, and nation, scattered throughout the world, worshiping Him in spirit and truth, working for Him by the power of the Holy Spirit, and witnessing for Him through their worship and work.

For those who are in Christ, the true Israel, Peter applies to his readers then (and you and me now) the language that God used for the nation of Israel in the Old Testament. Peter refers to Isaiah's prophecy about Israel's only Savior, which is filled with language depicting God as the Redeemer, Savior, Holy One of Israel, Creator, and King (Isa. 43:1, 3, 14–15). It also describes God's people as those precious in His eyes, honored by Him, and loved by Him (Isa. 43:4). His people include sons and daughters from the ends of the earth (Isa. 43:6). Furthermore, it tells us that the Lord is doing a new thing (Isa. 43:19). Part of the new thing He was doing was giving refreshment to His chosen people whom He formed for Himself, so that they might declare His praise (Isa. 43:20–21). Peter refers to these latter verses when he calls his readers "a chosen race." Though they may be from all different tribes, tongues, and nations, they are one in Christ, chosen by God the Father before the foundation of the world.

The next three descriptions of believers are taken from Exodus 19:5–6, the context of which is Israel at the foot of Mount Sinai after their deliverance from Egypt and before receiving the Ten Commandments. God had redeemed them from Egypt in order to bring them to Himself and make them His treasured possession among all peoples of the earth, a kingdom of priests and a holy nation. Just as God had delivered Israel out of the darkness of Egypt into the light of a relationship with Him, so too Jesus has delivered Peter's readers (and us) out of the darkness of their sins into the light of His love and grace, fully reconciled to God.

37

Previous to Israel going into exile, the Lord sent the prophet Hosea to proclaim a message to His people. In language that portrays Israel as the wife and God as the husband, Hosea speaks a powerful word of judgment against Israel, who had been unfaithful to her covenant commitment. Yet, instead of disowning Israel, the Lord promised that He would take her back. The Lord had Hosea illustrate His grace in his own marriage relationship; Hosea's wife was a whore, and he gave the children she bore to him names that reflected God's relationship with Israel. The name of the second child was No Mercy, and the name of the third child was Not My People. Later, the Lord spoke a word of grace through Hosea:

> I will have mercy on her who had not obtained mercy;
> Then I will say to those who were not My people,
> "You are My people!"
> And they shall say, "You are my God!" (Hos. 2:23)

Peter quotes this verse in his letter, displaying the amazing grace that has come to his readers through Christ Jesus. They too had had many affairs with the gods of this world, acting in unfaithfulness to their Creator. Yet God chose them in Christ to be His people and to extend mercy to them. This is no less true for you and me today.

### Conclusion

What are you trying to make your cornerstone today—achievement, beauty, a career, drugs and alcohol, entertainment, family and friends, financial security, good works, health, love, money, relationships, sexual sin, worldly counsel, or _____ (you fill in the blank)? All of these things will cause our lives to be crooked and untrue.

Peter reminds us there is a better solution to leveling our crooked lives than what the world offers us. He teaches us that Christ alone must be our cornerstone in order for our hearts to be straightened out and made pure. He reminds us that such spiritual building is not accomplished apart from the community of believers. He encourages us by telling us that we will not be put to shame in the end. And he reminds us that we are part of a splendid heritage. We are a chosen generation, a royal priesthood, a holy nation, and His own special people. Let us come to Christ, the living stone, offering praises to Him and proclaiming the praises of His grace.

# Processing It Together...

1. What do we learn about God in 1 Peter 2:4–10?

2. How does this reshape how we should view our present circumstances?

3. What do we learn about God's Son, Jesus Christ?

4. How should this impact our relationship with God and with others?

5. What do we learn about God's covenant with His people?

6. How are we to live in light of this?

7. How can we apply 1 Peter 2:4–10 to our lives today and in the future?

8. How should we apply these verses in our churches?

9. Looking back at "Put It in Perspective" in your personal study questions, what did you find challenging or encouraging about this lesson?

10. Looking back at "Principles and Points of Application," how has this lesson impacted your life?

# Submitting as Servants, Sufferers, and Spouses

1 Peter 2:11–3:7

## Purpose...

**Head.** What do I need to know from this passage in Scripture?

- Jesus Christ, the Suffering Servant, is the paradigm for all Christians to follow as they live their lives as strangers in this world, submitting to authority for the sake of kingdom witness.

**Heart.** How does what I learn from this passage affect my internal relationship with the Lord?

- I am a kingdom disciple who lives as a servant of God as I willingly submit to those in authority over me so that I might be a witness for Christ.

**Hands.** How does what I learn from this passage translate into action for God's kingdom?

- I will keep my conduct among unbelievers honorable.
- I will live as a servant of God, serving others in humility and love.
- I will endure sorrow while suffering unjustly, following in Christ's steps.
- I will serve my husband in gracious and humble actions.
- I will pray for unbelievers, asking the Lord to save them.
- I will pray for my persecuted brothers and sisters in Christ, asking the Lord to strengthen them in their suffering.

# Personal Study...

**Pray.** Ask that God will open up your heart and mind as you study His Word. This is His story of redemption that He has revealed to us, and the Holy Spirit is our teacher.

**Ponder the Passage.** Read 1 Peter 2:11–3:7.

- *Point.* What is the point of this passage? How does this relate to the point of the entire book?

- *People.* Who are the main people involved in this passage? What characterizes them?

- *Persons of the Trinity.* Where do you see God the Father, God the Son, and God the Holy Spirit in this passage?

- *Puzzling Parts.* Are there any parts of the passage that you don't quite understand or that seem interesting or confusing?

**Put It in Perspective.**

- *Place in Scripture.* Since you have studied 1 Peter's place in Scripture in lesson 1, you may want to take this opportunity to review your answer.

*The following questions will help if you got stuck on any of the previous questions, and they will help you dig a little deeper into the text, putting it all into perspective.*

**1. 2:11–12.** (a) Why can believers be called "Beloved" (see Mark 1:11; 9:7)?

(b) Who has made believers "sojourners and pilgrims," or exiles (1:1–2)?

(c) Read Genesis 23:4. Who is speaking in this verse, and what circumstance do Peter's readers share with him? Think of Israel's history. What do the readers share in common with Israel?

(d) Why are Peter's readers to abstain from the passions of the flesh?

(e) Why do fleshly lusts wage war against the believer's soul (Gal. 5:16–24)?

(f) Why are Peter's readers to keep their conduct among the Gentiles honorable?

(g) How does this reflect Jesus's teaching (Matt. 5:16; see also James 3:13)?

(h) To what does the "day of visitation" refer (see Phil. 2:9–11; 1 Peter 1:5, 7, 13)?

**2. 2:13–17.** (a) To whom are we to submit, and why?

(b) Who ordains these authorities (see Rom. 13:1), and for what purpose?

(c) How does Peter define the will of God in these verses?

(d) How does this definition reflect Jesus's words in Matthew 5:16 and Luke 6:35, as well as Jeremiah's instruction in Jeremiah 29:7?

(e) What four specific imperatives (what we are to do) does Peter give his readers as a summary of submission?

(f) How do these reflect Mark 12:29–31?

**3. 2:18–20.** (a) How are servants to relate to their masters, and why are they to do this?

(b) How does Peter's instruction reflect Jesus's words in Matthew 5:43–48 and Luke 6:27–36?

**4. 2:21–25.** (a) According to Peter, what is the paradigm, or pattern, of the Christian life?

(b) Why are Christians called to suffer?

(c) What passage from the Old Testament does Peter quote regarding Christ's suffering? Why does he quote it here?

(d) How does Isaiah 53 reflect Leviticus 4:14–15; 17:11?

(e) How are we to live in light of Christ's death for our sins?

(f) Why was Christ's death on the tree a cursed death (see Deut. 21:22–23)?

(g) How is Christ our example, our Savior, our healer, our Shepherd, and the Overseer of our souls?

(h) Check the cross-references in your Bible and find some Old Testament passages that show that the imagery of the Lord being our Shepherd is rooted in them.

(i) How does Jesus continue to use this imagery (see Luke 15:1–7; John 10:1–18)?

**5. 3:1–6.** (a) To what does "likewise" refer?

(b) How are wives to relate to their own husbands?

(c) Why are Christian wives to submit to Christian husbands (see Eph. 5:22–24)?

(d) Why are Christian wives to submit to non-Christian husbands
(see 1 Peter 2:12, 15)?

(e) How should a wife adorn herself?

(f) How does this reflect 1 Samuel 16:7 and Proverbs 31:10–31?

(g) In verses 5–6, who does Peter give as examples for wives, and what did they do that makes them good examples (see Gen. 18:12)?

(h) How are Sarah's daughters to behave?

(i) How does 3:6 reflect Proverbs 3:25–27?

**6. 3:7.** (a) To what does "likewise" refer?

(b) How are husbands to live with their wives, and why?

(c) How does Ephesians 5:25–33 further instruct husbands on loving their wives?

**Principles and Points of Application.**

**7. 2:11–12.** (a) What fleshly lusts are waging war against your soul today?

(b) How are you putting these to death (see Gal. 5:16–25; Eph. 6:10–20; 2 Peter 1:3–5; 1 John 2:15–17)?

(c) Which of your family, friends, neighbors, or coworkers speaks against you because of your faith?

(d) How are you responding?

(e) How should you respond?

(f) What encouragement does verse 12 give you for responding with honorable conduct to those who oppose you?

**8. 2:13–17.** (a) How does it presently encourage you that the Lord ordains those who hold political offices?

(b) How do you subject yourself to the people in political offices in your speech, prayers, and conduct, so that others, especially unbelievers, notice your respect for their office?

(c) Spend time today praying for those holding political offices in your county, state, and country, asking the Lord to help them rule in righteousness and justice. Pray also for the salvation of unbelievers in those offices. And pray that those who are believers will be bold in their witness for Christ.

(d) How do you live in both freedom and servitude to God as you go about your daily routine?

(e) Is there someone you should be honoring, but you aren't? Ask the Lord to help you honor him or her.

(f) What brother or sister in Christ are you finding hard to love right now? Ask the Lord to give you His love for them.

(g) How are you showing that you fear God?

(h) How can you honor the leader of your country?

**9. 2:18–25.** (a) In what situation are you suffering unjustly?

(b) How does it encourage you that Christ, the Suffering Servant, who suffered on your behalf, is your leader, Savior, Shepherd, and the Overseer of your soul in the midst of the situation?

(c) Use 2:21–25 to write out a prayer of thanksgiving for who Christ is and what He has done for you.

**10. 3:1–6.** (a) If you are married to an unbeliever, how are you using your circumstance as an opportunity to be a witness for the Lord?

(b) If you are married to a believer, are you submitting to him? How are you doing this? How can you help him spiritually? How can you encourage him in his worship, work, and witness?

(c) If you are single, spend time in prayer for God's will to be done in your life regarding marriage. Also, pray for your friends who are married to unbelievers. Finally, spend time in prayer for those you know in troubled marriages.

(d) How much emphasis do you put on your outward appearance versus cultivating the beauty of a gentle and quiet spirit through the means of grace (studying the Word of God, partaking of the sacraments, praying, and fellowshipping with other believers)?

**11. 3:7.** (a) If you are married, spend time in prayer for your husband, praying that he will live with you in an understanding way and show honor to you.

(b) If you are not married, pray for your future husband (if it is the Lord's will that you marry), as well as the marriages of family and friends for which you feel led to pray.

# Putting It All Together...

It is presently estimated that there are more than one hundred thousand believers suffering unjust treatment in North Korea. Such a staggering number made quite an impression on my oldest son, who read about it in our church bulletin and heard of it from our pastor's prayer—so much so that for some time, every night at bedtime when I leaned over him to pray and ask him if he had any prayer requests, he asked me to pray for these one hundred thousand believers.

Such suffering is foreign to those of us who live in the West, and yet we are not immune. Slander from neighbors and coworkers, as well as ostracism from gatherings where we are not wanted because of what we believe, can be painful. Ridicule from our family members ricochets through our hearts, leaving its mark.

Such shame, slander, and ridicule has the potential to leave us hopeless, except when we turn our eyes to our Lord and Savior, the one in whose footsteps we are called to follow. Jesus knew shame like you and I will never know it. He knew slander and ridicule of the fiercest kind, such that you and I will never endure. Yet in it all, He willingly and freely submitted to God's will, bearing the sin of God's children in His body on the cross of Calvary. Such love calls us to follow in Christ's footsteps for a purpose, to glorify God as we worship Him, work for Him, and witness for Him in a hostile world.

Peter has much to say about suffering as we submit to those God has placed over us. Whether we are submitting to government authorities, employers, or spouses, our reason for submission remains the same. We have been called to live as people who are servants of God, willingly laying down our lives for the sake of gospel witness. In our words and most especially our works, we are to present a beautiful picture of the gospel to others so that they too might glorify God.

## I. Living as Strangers: Submitting as Servants (2:11–17)

In the previous section of his letter (1:1–2:10), Peter grounded us in who we are in Christ. In this second major section, which is signaled by the word "Beloved," he exhorts us how to live in light of whose we are and who we are. He has already combined these two truths at the beginning of his letter, referring to his readers as "pilgrims" who are "elect" (1 Peter 1:1–2). It is precisely because Peter's readers are elect (chosen by God) and citizens of another kingdom (the kingdom of God) that they are exiles on earth.

Peter writes as a pastor, calling his sheep "Beloved." Peter was well acquainted with this term. As he watched Jesus transfigured on the mountain, he heard the Father's voice say, "This is My beloved Son. Hear him!" (Mark 9:7). Only those who are in Christ (the firstborn beloved Son of God) can be called beloved. As Paul so eloquently says,

> Blessed be the God and Father of our Lord Jesus Christ, who has blessed us with every spiritual blessing in the heavenly places in Christ, just as He chose us in Him before the foundation of the world, that we should be holy and without blame before Him in love, having predestined us to adoption as sons by Jesus Christ to Himself, according to the good pleasure of His will, to the praise of the glory of His grace, by which He made us accepted in the Beloved. (Eph. 1:3–6)

The imagery of "sojourners and pilgrims" would have been familiar to Peter's readers. They came from a heritage of exile. Adam and Eve had been exiled from the garden of Eden after the fall. Abram had been called to leave his home and go to a place the Lord would show him, becoming a sojourner in the land (see Gen. 12:1–3; 23:4). Jacob and his sons, as well as their many descendants, spent four hundred years in the land of Egypt as slaves. Israel sojourned in the wilderness for forty long years before arriving in Canaan. Israel was exiled at the hand of enemies, and the Jews were dispersed as sojourners and exiles across a land that was not their home. Peter's readers were still scattered in a world that was not their home, living as strangers in a world that was hostile to Christians. But rather than be cause for despair, their status as strangers was to lead to strategic witness.

Their witness began with their worship. Before God, the Holy One of Israel who had called them to be His own, they were to live as children of obedience (1 Peter 1:14). As believers, they were new creatures in Christ, but they were not yet perfect creatures (not until glory will we be perfect). Not only was there hostility from without, but there was war within. Fleshly lusts were waging war against their souls. Peter's readers were well acquainted with fleshly lusts from their previous lifestyle as unbelievers (1 Peter 1:14), which included, though certainly were not limited to, "adultery, fornication, uncleanness, lewdness, idolatry, sorcery, hatred, contentions, jealousies, outbursts of wrath, selfish ambitions, dissensions, heresies, envy, murders, drunkenness, revelries, and the like" (Gal. 5:19–21). As those who had received an eternal inheritance and were children of the Holy One, they were now to live as such, with their lives characterized by the fruit of the Spirit: "love, joy, peace, longsuffering, kindness, goodness, faithfulness, gentleness, self-control" (Gal. 5:22–23).

Such honorable conduct, which is an act of worship, is Peter's audience's greatest witness. How they live before God (their worship) is their greatest testimony as they live before others (their witness). When the Gentiles, who spoke of them as "evildoers," witnessed their good deeds, their mouths would be stopped, and this witness may even win some of the Gentiles to Christianity. Regardless, on the final day of Christ's return, believers will be vindicated. Their good deeds will be glorified by all people, for every knee will bow and give glory to Jesus Christ and honor to His bride, the church, when He returns in glory (see Phil. 2:9–11; Rev. 6:9–11).

Peter's teaching is in keeping with Jesus's teaching to His disciples in His Sermon on the Mount. He instructed them, "Let your light so shine before men, that they may see your good works and glorify your Father in heaven" (Matt. 5:16). It is not easy to live a life of submission as strangers who are often slandered by others, yet that is exactly what the Lord calls us to do so that we might bring glory to Him. Such a purpose should motivate us to endure, but Peter gives us even more encouragement.

Peter reminded his readers that they were to submit themselves to "every ordinance of man" (2:13). Government rulers are made in God's image, and He sovereignly ordains them to hold the office of emperor or governor (see Rom. 13:1). In God's common grace, He uses even unbelieving rulers to restrain evil and to encourage good in this fallen world. Peter is speaking of government that is not abusing its power. There are times when we must say no to leadership and yes to God, but only when leadership asks us to specifically disobey God's word. Peter and the apostles had said this before the Jewish council when they were asked to stop teaching in Jesus's name: "We ought to obey God rather than men" (Acts 5:29).

God's will for His people is to live in submission to the authorities He has put in place. As unbelievers see God's people doing good, benefiting society at large, their slander will be silenced. Far from taking freedom away from His people, the Lord gives true freedom to His people by freeing them from slavery to sin into a new relationship with Him. As His people, we are truly free by His grace and are not to abuse such grace in licentious living. Instead, we are to use such freedom in living as servants of God, willingly and joyfully obeying His will.

Humble service that comes only from those who know who they truly are in Christ is to characterize God's people in their interactions with everyone. Peter tells us that we must fear God, our loving Master. We must fervently love the brotherhood, our fellow brothers and sisters in Christ who work for the same Master. We must honor our leaders, who are ordained by the Lord. And we must honor everyone since all people are made in the image of God.

Peter's words in these verses (2:13–17) reflect the prophet Jeremiah's words to the exiles in Babylon, "Seek the peace of the city where I have caused you to be carried away captive, and pray to the LORD for it; for in its peace you will have peace" (Jer. 29:7). Peter also reflects Jesus's teaching, "But love your enemies, do good, and lend, hoping for nothing in return; and your reward will be great, and you will be sons of the Most High. For He is kind to the unthankful and evil. Therefore be merciful, just as your Father also is merciful" (Luke 6:35–36). Though freedom and servanthood may sound like a contradiction, in God's kingdom the two go together. There was no one freer than the Son of God, and yet He came to serve. When Jesus picked up the towel to wash His disciples' feet, He showed them what it meant to be both free and a submissive servant (see John 13:1–17). Peter's four imperatives (what we are to do), which succinctly summarize subjecting ourselves to others in order to glorify God and witness for Him, reflect the two greatest commandments, to love the Lord with all our heart and to love our neighbor as ourselves (see Mark 12:29–31).

Peter's words challenge those of us today who have been raised to think of freedom as a right instead of a privilege. We may fight for freedom so that we can be whoever we want to be and do whatever we want to do, but God's Word reminds us that this is not true freedom. True freedom is found in Christ alone, the One who sets us free from fleshly lusts raging against our souls and gives us a new heart that places Him on the throne and enables us to love others, even at great cost to ourselves.

## II. Living as Strangers: Submitting as Sufferers (2:18–25)

In a culture that grounded the success of society in the foundation of the family, it is not surprising that Peter used the paradigm of the Greco-Roman household codes (how family members were to relate to one another according to the laws of the ancient Greeks and Romans) in his letter. However, it is imperative that we recognize he totally transformed the Greco-Roman code of conduct. For example, in the Greco-Roman world slaves and wives were given much less respect than Peter gives them, and both were expected to follow their master's or husband's god, an idea Peter refuses to advocate because God has chosen His children and called them to follow Him. Therefore, Peter's readers were to submissively operate within society where they could, but they were to always do so as God's people, following His code of conduct (the Word of God) as their final authority.

Although Peter specifically addressed servants in these verses, we will see that such servants become a paradigm for every Christian to follow. As we've already discussed, we are called to live as servants of God (2:16). Servants in Peter's day would have included people who in our day are considered professionals (estate managers, physicians, teachers, and tutors).[1] Peter exhorted servants to be respectfully submissive not only to good and gentle masters but also to unjust masters. Servants of God are able to

---

1. Clowney, *Message of 1 Peter*, 112.

bear unjust suffering because they know the grace of God, and they live in the light of being worshipers of Him, workers for His kingdom, and witnesses for Him. Enduring sorrow while suffering unjustly may lead to the salvation of a stern master (see 1 Peter 3:1–2). Suffering for doing good displays God's grace to the sinful party by giving them respect and service when they don't deserve it.[2]

Peter reminds his readers that their calling is rooted in Christ's example. He is the Suffering Servant of Isaiah 53 in whose footsteps we are to follow. Peter's language is laced with Isaiah 53, displaying Christ as the fulfillment of Isaiah's prophecy. First, Peter reminds his readers of Christ's life of obedience. He walked this earth as the sinless Son of God, living a life of perfect obedience on behalf of God's children. He continually entrusted Himself to His heavenly Father, the just judge, instead of taking vengeance on His enemies. Second, Peter reminds his readers of Christ's death. He bore our sins in His body on the tree, dying a cursed death (Deut. 21:22–23) in order to free God's children from the curse of sin and death. When Christ died, God's children died to sin. When Christ was raised to new life, God's children were raised to new life, so that they might live for righteousness. His death has healed us and brought us back from wandering as lost sheep to the true Shepherd and Overseer of our souls.

Isaiah wrote of Jesus using the imagery of a lamb that is led to the slaughter and a sheep that is silent before its shearers (Isa. 53:7). Such imagery is rooted in the sacrificial system of Israel, which pictured in many different ways Christ's future work of atonement (see Lev. 4:14–15; 17:11). He is the final sacrifice who atoned for the sins of God's people (see Heb. 10:1–18).

Not only is Christ the sheep but He is also the Shepherd. David spoke of Christ when he penned Psalm 23. Ezekiel also spoke of Christ as the future Shepherd who would come and deliver God's people from the wicked shepherds of Israel. Ezekiel prophesied that Christ would search for His sheep and seek them out. He would usher them into God's inheritance, bringing back the ones who strayed, binding up the injured, strengthening the weak, and feeding them with justice. He would be the servant of David, the shepherd of Israel, fulfilling the promises of God (see Ezek. 34:11, 13, 15–16, 23–24, 30–31). Zechariah also spoke of Christ as the coming Shepherd who would be struck, resulting in the scattering of God's sheep for the purpose of testing and refinement, resulting in a purified remnant (Zech. 13:7–9).

Jesus quoted Zechariah's prophecy before His death, indicating that He was the Shepherd who would be struck, but He also told His disciples that they would fulfill the prophecy of the sheep scattering. Jesus also spoke of himself as the Good Shepherd who lays down His life for the sheep (John 10:1–18). In the parable of the lost sheep, He taught the grumbling tax collectors and scribes that He is the one who came to seek and to save His lost sheep (Luke 15:1–7).

---

2. By saying this, I am in no way advocating that someone remain in an abusive situation. If you are being abused by someone, please seek the help of your pastors and elders immediately.

As those who are in Christ, we also are called to suffer as servants of God. Jesus teaches us that we must love not only our neighbors but also our enemies. We are to pray for our persecutors and give grace to those who refuse to extend grace to us (see Matt. 5:43–48; Luke 6:27–36). This is an incredibly difficult thing to do. But when we remember that Christ is not only our Shepherd but also the one who oversees our souls, we can take courage that He will uphold us and strengthen us in the midst of suffering, so that we might bring glory to our Father in heaven.

### III. Living as Strangers: Submitting as Spouses (3:1–7)

Peter continues transforming the typical Greco-Roman household code, employing its paradigm for his purposes. He began this section of his letter (2:11–4:11) by reminding us that we are the beloved of God who are strangers in this world, and continued by teaching us that we are also servants of God who must freely and graciously submit ourselves to others so that we might be a witness to them of God's loving-kindness and grace. After an introduction (2:11–17), he specifically addressed servants (2:18–25), using the paradigm of Christ the Suffering Servant to solidify his point. Now, in these verses, he specifically addresses spouses, beginning with the wife and moving to the husband.

Peter exhorts wives to be subject to their own husbands. In keeping with his primary concern in this section of his letter—being a good witness to unbelievers so that they might see our good works and glorify God (2:12, 15)—Peter specifically addresses wives of unbelieving husbands (although his principles certainly apply to a marriage of two believers as well). Peter knows there is a time to proclaim the word of God with words, but here he emphasizes the need to proclaim the word of God with good works. As a believing wife lives with her unbelieving husband in respectful and pure ways, she may win him to Christ without a word. Even if he doesn't become a believer, he may respect his wife's conduct and show her favor instead of ridiculing her. This is not a blanket promise, but it is an encouragement to wives to seek to win their husband by good works instead of great words.

While she is not to be unkempt in appearance, a Christian wife is to emphasize and prioritize the inward beauty of the heart. Such beauty never fades, unlike our outward appearance, which gives way to white hair and wrinkles over time. In God's sight, it is the heart characterized by gentleness and quietness that is precious (see also 1 Sam. 16:7).

Peter draws on the example of Abraham's wife Sarah to emphasize the point that those who hope in God adorn themselves differently from those who submit to the standards of the world. Sarah displayed her respect to Abraham by calling him "lord," which was a term similar to our "Mr." today (see Gen. 18:12). Peter urges believers who are wives to be like the holy women of past generations who hoped in God by doing good and by living without fear. Peter alludes to Proverbs 3:25–27:

Do not be afraid of sudden terror,
Nor of trouble from the wicked when it comes;
For the LORD will be your confidence,
And will keep your foot from being caught.
Do not withhold good from those to whom it is due,
When it is in the power of your hand to do so.

The love of God casts out the fear of man. As we suffer, whether it is under unjust masters (1 Peter 2:18) or unbelieving husbands, we endure by keeping our eyes on Christ, the Suffering Servant who is our Savior, knowing that as we worship Him we are being a witness to the glory of God in this world. Our hope is not in our husband changing but in the Lord, who has the power to change our husband. We must constantly encourage women who are married to unbelievers to leave the work of salvation to the Lord and to take up the work of a quiet and gentle witness within her home.[3]

These verses also remind those of us who live in a day when beauty and youth are regarded as the greatest virtues; when billions of dollars are spent on advertising for plastic surgery, dieting, and fitness; and when billboards and magazines uphold picture-perfect models as the standard for all women, that God's Word defines beauty differently. Our time spent searching the Scriptures, praying, attending church, and fellowshipping with other believers should far outweigh our time spent on doing our hair and makeup, jogging, and shopping.

Peter also has a word for husbands, which is another example of how he heightens and transforms the Greco-Roman household codes. Peter calls husbands to live with their wives in an understanding way. Husbands should seek to learn about their wives, gaining understanding of who they are over the course of their marriage relationship. A husband is to show honor to his wife, the weaker vessel. The latter term mainly refers to physical strength but also to social status in Peter's day. It certainly does not refer to a woman's worth (see Gal. 3:28–29). Peter quickly guards against the latter interpretation by saying that wives are fellow heirs with their husbands of the grace of life. The Lord considers honor a husband shows to his wife so important that Peter warns the men of hindered prayer if they refuse to live with their wives in a gracious way.

In a day when marriage and family life are under attack, the Word of God offers hope. Peter tells us who we are in Christ and how we are to live in light of that identity. Far from following ten steps to a better marriage, we follow Christ, the Suffering Servant, the Shepherd and Overseer of our souls, who enables us to live as worshipers of Him in our home, workers for Him as we serve our spouses and families, and witnesses for Him as we proclaim the gospel in actions that beautifully reflect the grace of God.

Perhaps you are enduring shame, slander, and ridicule today at the hands of leaders, coworkers, or your spouse. Maybe you have lost hope that you can continue to

---

3. Again, Peter is not addressing abusive marriages in these verses. If you are in an abusive relationship, please immediately seek the help of your local pastors, elders, or deacons.

endure. Peter gives us a word of hope by proclaiming to us the kingdom of God and teaching us about Jesus Christ, the Suffering Servant, in whose footsteps we are privileged to follow. Jesus, our Good Shepherd, will carry us through such times of shame, slander, and ridicule. He will bind up our wounds and heal our broken heart. As the Overseer of our soul, He will guard our heart and protect us from the slander of man. In our home, He will strengthen us to carry on, praying for our husband and serving him even if he despises our faith. He will enable us to bear up under the slander of our neighbors without speaking badly of them. And He will encourage us as we suffer in the workplace for His glory, letting our light shine before others so that they may see our good works and glorify God. We can persevere because Jesus has suffered for us. He is our guide, our life, our Savior, our Shepherd, our Overseer, and the husbandman of our souls. We are safe and secure in Him.

## Processing It Together...

1. What do we learn about God in 1 Peter 2:11–3:7?

2. How does this reshape how we should view our present circumstances?

3. What do we learn about God's Son, Jesus Christ?

4. How should this impact our relationship with God and with others?

5. What do we learn about God's covenant with His people?

6. How are we to live in light of this?

7. How can we apply 1 Peter 2:11–3:7 to our lives today and in the future?

8. How should we apply these verses in our churches?

9. Looking back at "Put It in Perspective" in your personal study questions, what did you find challenging or encouraging about this lesson?

10. Looking back at "Principles and Points of Application," how has this lesson impacted your life?

# Called to Righteousness
# and Reconciliation

1 Peter 3:8–4:11

## Purpose...

**Head.** What do I need to know from this passage in Scripture?

- Jesus Christ, who became to me righteousness from God and reconciled me to Him, calls me to renounce ungodliness and reflect God's grace.

**Heart.** How does what I learn from this passage affect my internal relationship with the Lord?

- I am a kingdom disciple who rests in Christ's righteousness and reconciling work on my behalf while I renounce ungodliness and reflect God's grace to those around me.

**Hands.** How does what I learn from this passage translate into action for God's kingdom?

- I will extend unity, sympathy, love, tenderness, and humility to those around me.
- I will humbly and respectfully explain the reason for the hope that is within me to those who ask me about my faith.
- I will pray for the Lord to save my unsaved family, friends, and neighbors.
- I will help others prepare for suffering and endure it when it comes.
- I will extend hospitality to others without grumbling.
- I will glorify God and serve the church with my spiritual gifts.

# Personal Study...

**Pray.** Ask that God will open up your heart and mind as you study His Word. This is His story of redemption that He has revealed to us, and the Holy Spirit is our teacher.

**Ponder the Passage.** Read 1 Peter 3:8–4:11.

- *Point.* What is the point of this passage? How does this relate to the point of the entire book?

- *People.* Who are the main people involved in this passage? What characterizes them?

- *Persons of the Trinity.* Where do you see God the Father, God the Son, and God the Holy Spirit in this passage?

- *Puzzling Parts.* Are there any parts of the passage that you don't quite understand or that seem interesting or confusing?

**Put It in Perspective.**

- *Place in Scripture.* Since you have studied 1 Peter's place in Scripture in lesson 1, you may want to take this opportunity to review your answer.

*The following questions will help if you got stuck on any of the previous questions, and they will help you dig a little deeper into the text, putting it all into perspective.*

1. **3:8–12.** (a) How does 3:8–9 both conclude the previous section and introduce the next one?

(b) From the context of Peter's letter, how would you define being of one mind, having compassion, loving as brothers, being tenderhearted, and being courteous?

(c) Instead of returning evil for evil, what does Peter call his readers to do, and why?

(d) Check the cross-references in your Bible to see which Old Testament passage Peter is quoting in 3:10–12. How does it support his thoughts in verses 8–9?

(e) Since Peter has referred to Psalm 34 often in his letter, it would be a good time to read the entire psalm as well as its background in 1 Samuel 21:10–15.

(f) How is Jesus the fulfillment of Psalm 34:12–16?

(g) How do Jesus's words in Matthew 5:3–12; Luke 6:27–28; and 10:25–37 reflect the psalmist's words?

**2. 3:13–17.** (a) In light of Psalm 34:12–16, what is the answer to Peter's question in 3:13 (see also Rom. 8:35–39)?

(b) How does Peter show in 3:14 he is not teaching that Christians will live a life free of harm on this side of glory?

(c) Look up Isaiah 8:12. What is the context of this verse? Why does Peter quote this verse in 3:14b?

(d) How do we combat the fear of man?

(e) Why is it important to answer those who ask us for a reason for the hope that is in us with meekness and fear?

(f) Why is it important that believers have a good conscience?

(g) How does Peter teach that God is sovereign over our suffering?

(h) How do Peter's words in these verses reflect Jesus's words (see Matt. 5:10–12, 29; 10:28; John 3:20; 15:19; 16:33; 17:15)?

3. **3:18.** (a) How does Peter use Christ's suffering to prove his point that "it is better, if it is the will of God, to suffer for doing good than for doing evil" (3:17)?

(b) How many times did Christ suffer for sins (see also Heb. 10:8–14)?

(c) How did Christ suffer as the just for the unjust (see also Rom. 5:18–21)?

(d) How has Christ brought us to God (see Rom. 5:6–11; 2 Cor. 5:16–21; Col. 1:21–23)?

(e) To what event does "put to death in the flesh" refer?

(f) To what event does "made alive by the Spirit" refer?

**4. 3:19–20.** These verses are known as some of the most difficult to understand in the New Testament. For background, read Genesis 6–9. It may help you to think through the following as you seek to understand these verses: Where did Christ go? When did Christ go? To whom did Christ go? Why did Christ go?

**5. 3:21–22.** (a) To what does baptism correspond?

(b) What is the purpose of baptism? You may also want to refer to the Westminster Confession of Faith, chapter 28; Westminster Larger Catechism, questions 165–67; Westminster Shorter Catechism, questions 94–95; the Heidelberg Catechism, questions 69–74; or the Belgic Confession, article 34.[1]

(c) What language does Peter use to move from Christ's death to His resurrection to His ascension in 3:18–22?

(d) Where is Christ now, and who is subject to Him?

**6. 4:1–6.** (a) Why should believers expect suffering?

(b) How do believers prepare for it?

(c) How do Christians live in light of the gospel (see also Rom. 6:8–12)?

---

1. The Westminster Standards can be found at http://www.pcaac.org/resources/wcf/. The Heidelberg Catechism and the Belgic Confession can be found at http://www.urcna.org/1651/file_retrieve/23908 and http://www.urcna.org/1651/file_retrieve/23907, respectively.

(d) How does Peter characterize Gentiles?


(e) How do the Gentiles respond to believers?


(f) What encouragement does Peter give his readers as they suffer the criticism of the Gentiles with regard to God (4:5) and to believers of past ages (4:6)?


**7. 4:7–11.** (a) How do these verses reflect 2:11–12 and close the middle section of the letter (2:11–4:11), which I have titled "Living as Strangers"?


(b) To what time does "the end of all things" refer?


(c) Why is it important to be serious and watchful?


(d) How are believers to love one another, and why?


(e) Check the cross-references in your Bible to see where the phrase "love will cover a multitude of sins" comes from in the Old Testament.


(f) How are believers to show hospitality? Why would believers be tempted to grumble while showing hospitality?

(g) Who has given us spiritual gifts, and for what purposes has He given them to us (one purpose relating to man and one to God)? How does He equip us to use them? For further study on spiritual gifts, see Romans 12:3–8; 1 Corinthians 12; and Ephesians 4:1–16.

(h) How do these verses reflect Jesus's teaching in Matthew 6:5–15; 18:21–22; and Luke 10:25–37?

**Principles and Points of Application.**

**8. 3:8–12.** (a) In what relationships are you lacking unity of mind? Compassion? Brotherly love? A tender heart? Courtesy? Confess these to the Lord and ask Him to help you display unity, compassion, love, tenderness, and courtesy.

(b) In what situation are you tempted to repay evil for evil right now? Confess this to the Lord and ask Him to help you bless your enemy, since you are blessed in Christ.

(c) How does it encourage you today that the eyes of the Lord are on the righteous and His ears are open to their prayer? Spend time in prayer today, praising the Lord for who He is and all that He has done.

**9. 3:13–17.** (a) What encouragements do you find in these verses?

(b) How do you honor Christ as holy in your heart?

(c) What do you say to people when they ask you to explain the reason for the hope within you?

(d) What is your attitude toward those who ask you about your faith? How do you speak with meekness and fear?

(e) In what ways are you presently suffering for doing good? How does it encourage you that God is sovereign over your suffering?

**10. 3:18–22.** (a) How do you live differently in light of Christ's death, resurrection, and ascension?

(b) How does God's patience in the days of Noah encourage you?

(c) How does God's judgment in the days of Noah also encourage you as you are tempted to repay evil for evil when others slander and shame you for your faith?

(d) In question 167, the Westminster Larger Catechism says we are to improve our baptism all our lives, especially during times of temptation and when we are witnessing the baptism of others. Read this question (see p. 63 for a link to the catechism if you don't have a copy). According to the catechism, how are we to improve our baptism? Are you doing this?

**11. 4:1–6.** (a) In what ways have you armed yourself with right thinking about suffering?

(b) How are you living for the will of God instead of for the lusts of men? In what areas do you still struggle with living for the lusts of men?

(c) How have you suffered criticism from others for not participating in worldly ways?

(d) How do verses 4–5 encourage you to leave judgment on your critics to the Lord?

(e) List believers of past generations who have been of particular encouragement to you in your Christian walk, and explain why.

(f) Consider beginning a prayer journal (if you don't already have one) to encourage the next generation of believers in your family to expect and to endure suffering as they read firsthand accounts of how you expected and endured it.

**12. 4:7–11.** (a) Spend time evaluating your prayer life today. How do you show both seriousness and watchfulness?

(b) Do you love to overlook an offense, or do you love to nurse an offense? Read 1 Corinthians 13. How does this passage both convict and encourage you?

(c) Who do you need to show hospitality to this week, and are you tempted to grumble about it instead of rejoicing in the opportunity?

(d) How are you using your spiritual gift(s) to both serve other believers and glorify God? How are you relying on God's strength instead of your own as you serve?

# Putting It All Together...

There are few things I dislike more in relationships than being at odds with another person. You know how it goes. A small spark starts a ferocious fire, ending in discord, impatience, unkindness, a hard heart, and a proud mind. Seeking peace and pursuing it is never the first thing on our minds; war is. We have buckled our boots and are ready to stomp on the other person. We have heralded the battle cry and are ready to list every past wrong they have done. We have taken up our rifles and are ready to shoot until they know that they will pay for their sin.

Thankfully, God's grace often intervenes, revealing our sinfulness and another way to deal with things—living righteously by seeking peace and pursuing it, thereby being a blessing to those around us. A small step toward the other person starts a forgiving fire, ending in unity, love, a tender heart, and a humble mind. Seeking peace and pursuing it takes center stage. This is not easy, but it is the Lord's way.

In this lesson's passage, Peter calls us to be strangers in this world by living in righteousness, extending reconciliation to others, renouncing ungodliness, and reflecting God's grace. His call is grounded in who we are. We are those robed in Christ's righteousness, reconciled by Christ's blood to our heavenly Father, recipients of everything we need to live a life of godliness and of God's grace.

## I. Living as Strangers: Called to Righteousness (3:8–17)

Peter has been addressing his readers as those living as strangers in Asia Minor. In the previous section (2:11–3:7), he urged them to submission as servants (2:11–17), as sufferers (2:18–25), and as spouses (3:1–7). Now, he both concludes that section and introduces a new one in 3:8–9: "Finally, all of you be of one mind, having compassion for one another; love as brothers, be tenderhearted, be courteous; not returning evil for evil or reviling for reviling, but on the contrary blessing, knowing that you were called to this, that you may inherit a blessing." It is difficult to have unity of mind, especially in a culture that promotes individual rights, but Christ calls us to unity because He has reconciled us to God. We are to live in sympathy with one another, recognizing one another as both sinners and sufferers, exhorting one another to turn away from sin, and encouraging one another to turn to God in the midst of suffering. We are to love one another as those who are blessed to be part of the family of God. Our love must reflect God's love, which is patient, kind, and selfless. Our hearts are to be tender toward one another, forgiving each other and bearing one another's burdens. Finally, we are to be courteous to one another, humbly recognizing that we are in desperate need of grace as we extend grace to others. The Holy Spirit forges such character traits in us, enables us to return evil with good, and restrains us from reviling when we are reviled.

Peter reminds us that our call to righteousness is grounded in the blessing we have received from God the Father, "who has blessed us with every spiritual blessing in the heavenly places in Christ" (Eph. 1:3). We have been freed from the powers of evil so that we no longer have to return evil for evil. Instead, Christ is our peace and calls us to pursue peace with others. We are dead to sin and alive to righteousness.

Peter grounds his exhortation in the words of David in Psalm 34. This is not the first time Peter has referred to this psalm. Its background is found in 1 Samuel during the days when David, after learning from Saul's son Jonathan that Saul was determined to kill him, fled to Nob and then on to Gath. Being recognized by the servants of Achish, David disguised himself as a madman (1 Sam. 21:10–15). Psalm 34 was penned in reflection of such suffering. It is significant then that Peter uses this background of David's life to encourage his readers, who are also suffering at the hand of their enemies.

In this psalm, David begins by blessing the Lord, who has blessed him (34:1–2). Then he calls others to join him in exalting the Lord's name (34:3). Next, he testifies to the Lord's deliverance (34:4–7) before exhorting his fellow believers to taste and see that the Lord is good by trusting in Him (34:8–10). Following this exhortation, he calls God's people to listen to him so that he might teach them the fear of the Lord (34:11). The next verses contain his teaching (34:12–16), which are the verses Peter quotes in 1 Peter 3:10–12. The psalm closes by reminding God's people that the Lord hears the righteous when they cry to Him and delivers them, but those who hate the righteous will be condemned (34:17–22). Now we are in a better position to see why Peter used this psalm so often in his letter to suffering servants of God living as strangers in Asia Minor. They needed to be reminded to fear the Lord, not man, and to trust that the Lord would deliver them from their enemies and judge their enemies for their injustice and wrongdoing.

The world was telling Peter's readers that loving life and seeing good days meant taking a dip in debauchery, but Peter reminded them that such disobedience did not hold a blessing. Instead, blessing is found in living a life of righteousness, which can be done only in Christ, who transforms us into new creatures with new hearts and who enables us to walk in goodness, truthfulness, peace, and righteousness. The eyes of the Lord are on believers because His eyes are on His Son, and we are in Christ. His ears are open to our prayers because Jesus lives to intercede for us, and the Spirit convicts us of our sin so that we might walk in fellowship with the Lord.

Peter reflects Jesus's own words in the Sermon on the Mount, which are known as the Beatitudes. Jesus reminds His listeners that although they endure all kinds of suffering for righteousness' sake on this side of glory, their reward in heaven is great (Matt. 5:3–12). That is why it is so important for us to keep our eyes fixed on Christ when others are not blessing us with kindness. When our eyes are on the One who has extended grace and mercy freely to us when we are so undeserving, we will then be able to extend grace and mercy to others.

Since the eyes of the Lord are on the righteous and the face of the Lord is against those who do evil, there is no one to harm those who are zealous for what is good—not ultimately, anyway. Peter knows that his readers will endure suffering for righteousness' sake, but it is in that suffering, not in spite of it, that blessing is found. It is the blessing of sharing in Christ's suffering (1 Peter 4:13), of having fellowship with the Lord, of having a heart filled with true peace, and of loving life because your life is Christ.

Honoring Christ in our hearts as holy drives out the fear of man, as well as the fear of troubles, and prepares us to tell others why we live in hope. The believer must speak in meekness and fear (respect) and with a clear conscience before God. Those who slander us when we are doing good to them will be put to shame. If we suffer, let us suffer for righteousness' sake, not for doing wrong. There will be times in our lives when God wills that we should suffer for doing good, and we can rest assured that it is always for His glory, our good, and the good of our neighbor. Our worship (honoring Christ as holy) is our greatest witness (handling others with meekness, respect, and a good conscience even when they treat us wrongfully).

In these verses Peter refers to Isaiah 8:12 (see 3:14–15), which in its original context speaks of the coming Assyrian invasion against the Northern Kingdom of Israel, which led to exile. Isaiah had a hard message to preach to a hard-hearted Israel, but the Lord encouraged him with these words:

> Do not say, "A conspiracy,"
> Concerning all that this people call a conspiracy,
> Nor be afraid of their threats, nor be troubled.
> The LORD of hosts, Him you shall hallow;
> Let Him be your fear,
> And let Him be your dread.
> He will be as a sanctuary,
> But a stone of stumbling and a rock of offense
> To both the houses of Israel,
> As a trap and a snare to the inhabitants of Jerusalem.
> And many among them shall stumble;
> They shall fall and be broken,
> Be snared and taken. (Isa. 8:11–15)

Jesus fulfilled this prophecy, which is why Peter says to honor Christ the Lord as holy. He is the stone of stumbling and rock of offense that Peter has already spoken of in his letter by quoting this verse in Isaiah (Isa. 8:14; 1 Peter 2:8).

Jesus teaches us that the wicked hate the light, wanting nothing to do with it, lest it expose their evil (John 3:20). He warned us that the world would hate us (John 15:19). He prepared us for tribulation in this world and encouraged us that He had overcome it and would give us His peace (John 16:33). He prayed that the Father would keep us from the Evil One, as we are strangers in this world (John 17:15).

Therefore, we should not lose heart but should honor Christ as holy in our hearts, anticipating slander and shame from our enemies and responding in meekness and respect. This can be done only by God's transforming grace at work within us. Left to ourselves, we would respond to evil with evil. But in Christ, we can respond with the love and righteousness of Christ, and in doing so we bring glory and honor to Him.

## II. Living as Strangers: Called to Reconciliation (3:18–22)

We are not merely called to righteousness as strangers in this world; we are also called to reconciliation. Throughout his letter Peter frequently grounds the imperatives (what we are to do) in the indicatives (what God has already done for us), specifically what Christ has done for us (see 1:18–21; 2:4–8, 21–25). Here again Peter grounds our suffering for righteousness' sake, which he has discussed in the previous verses (3:8–17), in the reconciliation Christ has accomplished for us, thereby calling us to a ministry of reconciliation as well (see Rom. 5:6–11; 2 Cor. 5:16–21; Col. 1:21–23). He begins by reminding us that Christ suffered once for sins. In contrast to the Old Testament sacrificial system, in which the blood of goats and rams had to be offered repeatedly to atone for man's sins and which was a shadow of the final sacrifice to come, Christ offered Himself as the final sacrifice, perfecting for all time those who are being sanctified (see Heb. 10:1–18). He suffered as the righteous God-man on behalf of the unrighteous who had been chosen by God before the creation of the world, reconciling us to God.

Although Christ died ("being put to death in the flesh"), He also rose again ("but made alive by the Spirit"). The Greek allows for the translation, "but made alive in *the Spirit, in whom* he went and proclaimed to the spirits in prison" (3:18–19, emphasis added), which lends support to the view, which I humbly hold, that the following verses are referring to the time of the flood, in which the Spirit of Christ preached a message of repentance through Noah to an unbelieving generation (those who are now "spirits in prison" awaiting God's condemnation on the final day of judgment) during the time he built the ark. Tragically, Noah's generation remained unrepentant, and only eight persons entered the ark by faith and were brought safely through the floodwaters.[2]

Peter teaches us how the story of Noah and the ark connects to the gospel by speaking of our baptism. The ark was a picture of the cross to come on which Jesus would die for our sins, atoning for them by bearing God's wrath for us. Our salvation is not just tied to Jesus's death, though; it is also, and more importantly, tied to His resurrection. Christ has reconciled us to God through His death and resurrection, a truth that our baptism not only symbolizes but also seals. Symbolically, our baptism

---

2. There are three main views, each with different modifications, that have been given to these verses over the course of church history. Edmund Clowney provides an excellent summary of these in his commentary. Clowney, *Message of 1 Peter*, 156–57.

displays that Christ has removed the sins from His people just as water removes dirt from the body. But baptism also seals to us as believers all the benefits that are now ours in Christ Jesus. We have been given a new name (baptized into the name of the Father, the Son, and the Holy Spirit). We have been given new life in Christ (united to Him in both His death and resurrection). And we have been given a new family (we are part of the family of God, the church of Christ).

Peter doesn't end this section with Christ's resurrection, but with His ascension. In these five verses he has moved us from Christ's death to His resurrection to His ascension. Peter's readers not only have a Savior who died for them and who was raised as the firstfruits of their resurrection, but they also have a Savior who has been exalted to the right hand of God the Father in heaven as King of kings and Lord of lords, with all angels, authorities, and powers (the very things that threaten to undo them, and now us) subjected to Him. Peter's encouragement could not be clearer. With a Savior who has not only died but has also been raised to new life and exalted to the heavens with all powers subjected to Him, there is no one and nothing that can harm his readers. Suffering may be the present word, but it is not the final word. Those who suffer with Him will also be glorified with Him, and that is the hope Peter's readers (and you and I) have been given.

As those who have been given this hope and who have been baptized into the name of the triune God, are united with Christ, and are brothers and sisters with one another, we have the tremendous privilege to live as strangers in this world with the ministry of reconciliation. Peter has taught us the fear of the Lord using Psalm 34 (3:10–12). Now we are to persuade others. We are ambassadors for Christ with God making His appeal to others through us. We are to implore others on behalf of Christ to be reconciled to God. We are to endure suffering for the sake of this ministry, proclaiming the day of salvation, just as Noah did in his day. Our mouths are to be open to others with the gospel message and our hearts wide open with Christ's love, as we proclaim the truth that God has reconciled us to Himself through Jesus Christ and has now given us the ministry of reconciliation (2 Cor. 5:18).

### III. Living as Strangers: Called to Renounce Ungodliness (4:1–6)

Since we are united to Christ and since Christ suffered in the flesh, we must also expect to suffer. Suffering is usually far greater for those who thought they could avoid it than it is for those who knew it would come one day and were mentally prepared for it. Crisis is certain to come. We must not think that something strange is happening when we suffer (1 Peter 4:12). This is the way of Christ—suffering first, then glory.

I remember when one of my pastors addressed the women of our church, reminding us that crisis was sure to come into our lives. We needed to be living in the midst of community, therefore, plugged in to our church instead of sitting on the sidelines. Community breathes life into crisis in many ways, not least of which is prayer. It has been a tremendous encouragement to me to see my church family come alongside those in deep suffering. The love of Christ that is poured out through His body by way of prayer, encouraging texts, e-mails, cards, meals, childcare, gift cards, and godly counsel is something unparalleled in other "communities." The love of Christ compels us to encourage one another, love one another, and support one another as we come together to renounce ungodliness and live out godly lives in the midst of suffering.

We are called to renounce ungodliness because we are in Christ. Since we died with Christ and He conquered sin, we have ceased from sin. The flesh no longer rules our lives; the Spirit does. We are new creatures with new hearts who are to live for the will of God. This does not mean that we will no longer sin. On this side of glory, the desires of the flesh are against the Spirit; they are opposed to each other as two enemies are opposed in war (Gal. 5:17–18).

Peter knows that his readers are well acquainted with the desires of the flesh. These desires characterized their lives before they became believers. In verse 3 he mentions six specific fleshly desires: sensuality ("lewdness"), passions ("lusts"), drunkenness, orgies ("revelries"), drinking parties, and lawless ("abominable") idolatry. Peter's readers were in a situation where their former drinking buddies still wanted them to drink. They were surprised that their Christian friends were no longer willing to join them in the flood of debauchery, and they were critical of them. What these "Gentiles" didn't realize was that their friends answered to a new judge, the judge of the living and the dead, not the judge of a fallen conscience that says, "Anything goes." The believers had been called to renounce ungodliness, not relish it.

Peter encourages his readers by reminding them that they are not experiencing anything new. The same gospel that they now held so dearly had also been preached to believers who had already died, perhaps for their faith. Though they were judged in the flesh during their lifetime, just as Peter's readers were being judged, they lived in the spirit the way God does, which is a life of hope grounded in the security of God's salvation.

I have known the pain of rejection for not doing "what everyone else does." It is hard to be like a fish swimming upstream. Ridicule, shame, and unkind gestures and remarks threaten to undo us if we fear man. But if we fear God and turn our eyes to Him for the strength to live lives that renounce ungodliness, we will find that He is more than able and more than willing to supply us with the grace that we need to continue renouncing ungodliness. As we pray for those who criticize us for not being any fun because we won't take part in the flood of debauchery with them, we will have hearts of compassion, not judgment, hoping that the Lord will save them as He has saved us.

## IV. Living as Strangers: Called to Reflect God's Grace (4:7–11)

Peter calls us to live in light of the end of all things because the end has already begun. Christ has already come and inaugurated His kingdom, but He is coming again to consummate it. In light of our place in redemptive history, we are to live prayer-filled lives. That means we need to be self-controlled and sober-minded so that we are able to pray. A sloppy stupor doesn't lead to a steady life of supplication, which we desperately need if we are going to reflect God's grace.

Prayer humbles us. It reminds us that we are absolutely dependent on someone other than ourselves for everything. Prayer teaches us. It teaches us that we are not the center of the universe; God is. Prayer encourages us. It enables us to rest in the sovereign plan of our heavenly Father. Prayer corrects us. It brings us in line with God's will. Prayer trains us. It focuses our eyes on things above, our hearts on Christ, and directs our hands to serve our neighbor. Prayer is where I turn first when I am suffering. By God's grace I have come to learn that there is no safer place to be than in communion with my Father when the storms of life come my way. As I cry out to Him in the midst of trials, He hides me under the shelter of His wings.

Jesus taught us how to pray. He taught us to approach God as His children, calling him Father. At the same time, He taught us to approach God as holy. He taught us to be kingdom-minded, desiring God's kingdom and will to be done on earth as it is in heaven. He taught us to rely on the Lord for each day's resources. He taught us to ask for forgiveness of our sins. Finally, He taught us to pray that He would keep us from the Enemy (Matt. 6:5–13).

Not only are we to reflect God's grace in our relationship with the Lord through prayer, we are also to reflect His grace in our relationship with others through love, hospitality, and service. First, we are to love our brothers and sisters in Christ earnestly. Think of something in your life that you have earnestly desired. Maybe it was a scholarship to a school, a relationship that would end in marriage, the blessing of children, or a particular job. Recall the earnestness you felt as you longed for the fulfillment of your dream. That is the earnestness we are to have when it comes to loving God's people. Peter reminds us that earnest love covers a multitude of sins, a reflection of Proverbs 10:12: "Hatred stirs up strife, but love covers all sins." We don't cover our brother's sin in the sense of forgetting and forgiving sins (only God can do that), but in the sense of being quick to overlook an offense for the sake of unity in the body of Christ. This doesn't mean we let all things go—some sin needs to be addressed—but it means we let several things go as we acknowledge that we are too often guilty of holding others to higher standards than we have for ourselves. When Peter asked Jesus how many times he had to forgive his brother, he set the bar too low. I imagine Peter thought he was being gracious to mention the number seven. But Jesus replied by raising the bar. We should be willing to forgive others seventy times seven (Matt. 18:21–22). In other words, we should reflect the forgiveness of our Savior, who has removed our sins as far as the east is from the west (see Ps. 103:12).

Second, we are to show hospitality to others without grumbling. Opening up our homes and our resources to others often seems easy at the beginning, but as their stay grows long and our resources are spent, we often grumble. We didn't really want these people to stay that long in our home after all. Chaos replaces our calm, and we are tempted to complain. Contrarily, hospitality is to reflect God's grace. We should extend our hands in hospitality because Christ extended His hands to us.

Jesus powerfully teaches us about hospitality in the parable of the good Samaritan (Luke 10:25–37). We are to show compassion to others, even at great cost to ourselves. Hospitality is a mercy ministry. The Lord will bring people who are in need into our lives, and we are to extend our hands toward them in mercy and compassion.

Third, we are to reflect God's grace by serving one another with the gifts He has given to us. Serving one another with our gifts stewards what God has given to us. He has gifted some to speak the Word of God. He has gifted others to minister. The gifts He has given are not limited to just these two (see Rom. 12:3–8; 1 Corinthians 12; Eph. 4:1–16). The different gifts among God's people reflect His creativity as well as His grace. Regardless of what gifts we have received, they are all undergirded by the strength that God supplies, so that He is glorified through Jesus Christ in everything we do. The glory and dominion do not belong to us, but to Him.

The celebrity teacher or preacher has often taken center stage in our churches today, replacing Christ. The glory goes to the best speaker, author, and teacher as they dominate the evangelical landscape around them. This should not be. We must not increase while Christ decreases. He must be preeminent in all things. One of my prayers before I teach is, "Father, help me to be a good steward of the platform You have given me today. Help me to show them Your Son, not Sarah."

The key to seeking peace and pursuing it is found only in Christ, who is our peace. He has pursued us, reconciling us to God. We love because He first loved us. We have tender hearts toward others because He was first tender toward us. We have a humble mind because He first humbled Himself for us. We forgive because He first forgave us. We show hospitality without grumbling to others because He first showed hospitality to us. We serve others because He first served us. In everything, we are to glorify God through Jesus Christ, because to Him alone belong the glory and dominion forever.

# Processing It Together...

1. What do we learn about God in 1 Peter 3:8–4:11?

2. How does this reshape how we should view our present circumstances?

3. What do we learn about God's Son, Jesus Christ?

4. How should this impact our relationship with God and with others?

5. What do we learn about God's covenant with His people?

6. How are we to live in light of this?

7. How can we apply 1 Peter 3:8–4:11 to our lives today and in the future?

8. How should we apply these verses in our churches?

9. Looking back at "Put It in Perspective" in your personal study questions, what did you find challenging or encouraging about this lesson?

10. Looking back at "Principles and Points of Application," how has this lesson impacted your life?

# The Creator God, the Chief Shepherd, and the Caring God

## 1 Peter 4:12–5:14

## Purpose...

**Head.** What do I need to know from this passage in Scripture?

- The Creator God is more than worthy of my trust as I suffer on this side of glory because He loves me and cares for me.

**Heart.** How does what I learn from this passage affect my internal relationship with the Lord?

- I am a kingdom disciple who entrusts my soul to the Creator God, others' souls to the Chief Shepherd, and my struggles to the caring God.

**Hands.** How does what I learn from this passage translate into action for God's kingdom?

- I will help others recognize suffering for Christ's name as a blessing.
- I will pray for my family, friends, and neighbors who are in need of salvation.
- I will pray for the pastors, elders, and other leaders of my church this week.
- I will help others cast their cares upon the Lord.
- I will help others stand firm in their faith.
- I will pray for my persecuted brothers and sisters in Christ.
- I will declare the true grace of God to those I encounter this week.

# Personal Study...

**Pray.** Ask that God will open up your heart and mind as you study His Word. This is His story of redemption that He has revealed to us, and the Holy Spirit is our teacher.

**Ponder the Passage.** Read 1 Peter 4:12–5:14.

- *Point.* What is the point of this passage? How does this relate to the point of the entire book?

- *People.* Who are the main people involved in this passage? What characterizes them?

- *Persons of the Trinity.* Where do you see God the Father, God the Son, and God the Holy Spirit in this passage?

- *Puzzling Parts.* Are there any parts of the passage that you don't quite understand or that seem interesting or confusing?

**Put It in Perspective.**

- *Place in Scripture.* Since you have studied 1 Peter's place in Scripture in lesson 1, you may want to take this opportunity to review your answer.

*The following questions will help if you got stuck on any of the previous questions, and they will help you dig a little deeper into the text, putting it all into perspective.*

**1. 4:12–13.** (a) How are Christians to respond to trials?

(b) What is the purpose of trials in the Christian life?

**2. 4:14–16.** (a) How does reproach for the name of Christ reveal that we are blessed?

(b) What kind of suffering does not result in glorifying God?

(c) What should not characterize us when we suffer as Christians?

(d) Read Isaiah 11:1–2. How does Christ fulfill this prophecy?

(e) How does Peter apply this passage to Christians?

**3. 4:17–19.** (a) What is the purpose of God's judgment among believers (see Mal. 3:1–3)?

(b) How does judgment begin on this side of glory?

(c) What will the purpose of God's judgment be among unbelievers at His second coming (2 Thess. 1:7–8)?

(d) What is Peter communicating to his readers when he quotes Proverbs 11:31?

(e) Why does Peter say that the righteous are "scarcely saved"? Is he saying that Christ's work is not adequate? Explain.

(f) What comforting truths does Peter remind us of in 4:19, and what does he exhort us to do in light of them?

**4. 5:1–3.** (a) Who does Peter exhort in these verses?

(b) How does Peter describe himself (see also John 21:15–19)?

(c) What are the elders to do, and how are they to do it?

(d) Look up the following Old Testament passages that use the imagery of shepherding for leadership among God's people: Genesis 49:24; 2 Samuel 5:2; Isaiah 53:6–7; Jeremiah 3:15; 23:1–4; and Ezekiel 34. What do you learn about shepherding from these passages?

(e) How does Peter's exhortation reflect Jesus's words in Mark 10:42–45 and His example as recorded in John 13:1–20?

**5. 5:4.** (a) How is Jesus, the Chief Shepherd, the fulfillment of the shepherd motif in the Old Testament (see Ps. 23; John 10:1–18)?

(b) What will the elders receive when the Chief Shepherd appears?

(c) How do Psalm 21:1–7; Isaiah 28:5; and Revelation 4:10 help illuminate what this crown of glory is and the purpose of it?

**6. 5:5.** (a) How does this verse continue Peter's thought in 2:13–3:8?

(b) Check the cross-references in your Bible. What Old Testament and New Testament passages is Peter reflecting in this verse?

**7. 5:6–7.** (a) Under whose hand are believers to humble themselves?

(b) How does Peter describe God's hand (see also Ex. 13:3; Deut. 9:26; Ezek. 20:33–44)?

(c) Why should believers humble themselves under God's hand?

(d) Why should we cast all our anxieties on God (see also Ps. 55:22)?

(e) How do Peter's words reflect Jesus's words (see Matt. 6:25–34; Mark 4:18–19)?

**8. 5:8–9.** (a) Why does Peter exhort believers to be sober and vigilant?

(b) How are we to resist the Enemy (see also Eph. 6:10–20)?

**9. 5:10–11.** (a) What hope do we have in the midst of our suffering?

(b) In verse 11, what is the result of Peter's understanding of God's grace?

**10. 5:12–14.** (a) What do we learn about Silvanus (Silas) from other parts of the New Testament (see Acts 15:22–23, 32, 40; 2 Cor. 1:19)?

(b) How does Peter describe him in these verses?

(c) How does Peter summarize his reason for writing this letter?

(d) Who sends greetings to Peter's readers?

(e) What do we know about the word "Babylon" from Revelation 14:8; 16:19; 17:5; and 18:2, 10?

(f) What else do we know about Mark (John Mark, sometimes simply John or Mark) from the New Testament (see Acts 12:12, 25; 13:13; 15:36–39; Col. 4:10; 2 Tim. 4:11)?

(g) How does Peter exhort his readers to greet one another when they are gathered for worship and hearing his letter?

(h) What does he extend to his readers, and how does this reflect Jesus's words in John 14:27?

**Principles and Points of Application.**

**11. 4:12–13.** (a) Briefly describe a time when you have been surprised by suffering.

(b) How would your suffering have looked different if you had recognized it as an opportunity to follow in Christ's steps and for the strength of your faith to be revealed?

(c) What suffering are you experiencing at present, and how are you responding to it?

**12. 4:14–16.** (a) How have you been insulted for the name of Christ?

(b) What encouragement can you take from verse 14 when you are insulted in this way?

(c) When you read the list of sins in verse 15, remember that the spirit of the law goes much deeper than the surface requirements. For example, Jesus explains the meaning of murder in the Sermon on the Mount, reminding us that if we are even angry with someone we have committed murder (see Matt. 5:21–26). In view of that understanding, how are you suffering today for sins that you need to repent of before the Lord?

(d) How are you glorifying God as a Christian in the midst of a culture that is becoming increasingly intolerant to Christianity?

**13. 4:17–19.** (a) In what ways is the Lord refining and purifying your heart right now? Spend time thanking Him that Christ has been judged for you so that the purpose of His discipline is to sanctify you instead of punish you.

(b) Spend time in prayer for family, friends, and neighbors you know who are not saved, asking the Lord to save them.

(c) What encouragement do you glean from verse 19 about suffering?

(d) How are you entrusting your soul to our faithful Creator while doing good?

14. **5:1–5.** (a) Use these verses to pray for the pastors and elders of your church daily this week.

(b) If you have been placed in a leadership role as a parent, a children's ministry worker, a women's ministry worker, or some other position of leadership, what guidance do these verses give you for shepherding those under your care?

(c) How does knowing that you serve others as one serving under the Chief Shepherd, Jesus Christ, change the way you serve?

(d) How do you display your submission to the elders and other leaders of your church?

(e) How are you clothing yourself with humility as you interact with others?

15. **5:6–7.** (a) In what areas of your life are you proud? Ask God to replace your pride with humility that comes from absolute dependence upon Him.

(b) In what areas of your life are you anxious? Ask our heavenly Father to replace your anxiousness with peace that comes from rest and trust in His care.

**16. 5:8–9.** (a) How are you watchful of the Enemy?

(b) How are you standing firm in your faith?

(c) How do verses 9–10 encourage you in your suffering?

**17. 5:10–11.** (a) What is your response to God's grace in your life?

(b) What encouragement does verse 10 offer you in your suffering?

**18. 5:12–14.** (a) To whom do you need to testify about the true grace of God today?

(b) How do you warmly greet your brothers and sisters in Christ on the Lord's Day?

(c) To whom do you need to extend peace?

# *Putting It All Together . . .*

I held her as she shook with sobs. She had called, asking if she could come to my home. It was evident she was in need of a word of hope, peace, and love in the midst of deep suffering. I had walked a hard road with her for many months, grieving alongside her as she endured suffering at the hand of another. Repeatedly, I had to urge her to entrust her soul to the God who made her and cared for her. I was only a shepherdess serving under the Chief Shepherd, pointing her toward Him, the One who could restore, confirm, strengthen, and establish her.

During those days I had the privilege of working as part of a team as I shepherded this woman through a crisis. The team was comprised of another woman and me as well as pastors and elders; it was small enough to respect confidentiality yet large enough to reflect the responsibility that the church had to care for this hurting soul. Over the months I came to deeply appreciate that I was not alone in shepherding her but was under the oversight of some of my pastors and elders. I was also stretched in my calling to shepherd my sister willingly, eagerly, and humbly, as there were moments when the timing was inconvenient and the burden too great to bear.

Peter was writing to people like you and me, people who were suffering. As a pastor and elder, he was a shepherd of sheep. In his closing section of his letter, he calls God's people to entrust their souls to God because He is the Creator God, to entrust others' souls to Him because He is the Chief Shepherd, and to entrust their struggles to Him because He is the caring God.

## I. Living as Sufferers: Entrusting Our Souls to the Creator God (4:12–19)

Peter begins his final section of the letter with these verses, signaled by the word "Beloved," which also conveys his deep pastoral care and tone. He too had suffered for Christ's name (see Acts 12:1–19), but he had also known what it was to suffer because he had denied Christ's name (see Mark 14:66–72). He doesn't want his readers to be surprised at the fiery trials in their lives. Unexpected suffering is even worse than expected suffering. He wants them to know that trials are tests sent by the faithful Creator to refine and purify His people, making them more and more like Christ. In fact, he wants them to rejoice not in spite of, but because of their suffering for Christ. They are to look back at Christ's suffering at the hands of men during His earthly life and rejoice that they follow in His footsteps. But they are also to look forward to Christ's glory, which was inaugurated at His resurrection and ascension and will be consummated at His second coming, knowing that they too will be glorified with Him. Present suffering pales in comparison to future glory, and they should readily endure it as they keep their eyes focused on their faithful Creator who will one day make all things new.

Peter reminds his readers that the insults they receive for being Christians confirm their Creator's faithfulness rather than bring it into question. Insults reveal that they are blessed people indeed because "the Spirit of glory and of God" rests upon them (v.

14). Peter takes his language from Isaiah 11:1–2, the context of which is God's glorious renewal of the faithful remnant of His people after exile. This renewal was related to His promise of a shoot from Jesse upon whom the Spirit of the Lord would rest, the Spirit of wisdom and understanding, counsel and might, knowledge and the fear of the Lord. Isaiah's prophecy found its fulfillment in Christ, upon whom the Spirit of God descended at His baptism and who was overshadowed with the cloud of glory at the transfiguration when the Father said, "This is My beloved Son. Hear Him!" (Mark 9:7). Incredibly, Peter now tells his readers that because they are in Christ, this same Spirit of glory and of God rests upon them.

Far from suffering as murderers, thieves, evildoers, or busybodies, the first three of which would bring the death penalty in their culture, Peter's readers were to suffer as Christians, which might also bring death. The Lord had already told Peter that he would die a martyr's death, and he had certainly experienced many occasions on which he could have died for his faith (Acts 5:17–42; 12:1–19). Suffering for our faith does not bring the shame that death from sin does. Contrarily, it would be his readers' glory to die because they glorify the Creator God in their death as Christians. Their death confirms their calling to follow in the footsteps of the One who had already died for them. Death would not be the final word. They will be raised with Him in glory while the whole world bows their knee to the Creator and Redeemer.

Suffering among God's people is simply the beginning of God's future judgment that will take place at the end times. At first glance, it doesn't make sense that God's people should be judged since Christ has taken God's judgment for them. But far from judgment that results in eternal separation from God in hell, as in the case of unbelievers (see 2 Thess. 1:7–8), God's judgment that begins with His household results in a refined people who are ready to meet their Creator when He comes (see Mal. 3:1–3). Such fatherly discipline proves His love for us, and our response proves our love for Him (see Heb. 12:3–11).

Peter quotes from Proverbs 11:31 to further his point. He argues that if the righteous are scarcely saved, the ungodly and the sinner have no hope. The righteous are not "scarcely saved" because their Savior's work is inadequate but because suffering is difficult and is part of their sanctification on this side of glory. The ungodly person, not willing to suffer for the name of Christ and rejecting His name altogether, has no hope of being saved because he or she has rejected the only hope of salvation—Jesus Christ the Lord. Because suffering is an intricate part of God's plan of salvation, as it progressively sanctifies us to be more like His Son and because we suffer under the hand of a faithful Creator, we are to entrust our souls to Him, resting in His promises to us, and we are to continue to do good in His name until He calls us home to glory.

Christ set this example for us throughout His entire earthly ministry. He continually entrusted His soul to His Father, trusting in His Father's will, surrendering to His Father's plan, and doing good to those around Him. We who are called to follow in His footsteps are to do the same. We serve a faithful Creator who is also our Redeemer. Not in spite of—but because of—our suffering we rejoice and rest in Him. We must not stuff our souls with the saviors of this world; rather, we are to entrust our souls to Him, our faithful Father. He has chosen us out of His mere grace and love to be His people, and He will not just deliver us from our suffering ultimately one day but will use our suffering in the process of sanctification so that we will be ready to meet His Son.

## II. Living as Sufferers: Entrusting Others' Souls to the Chief Shepherd (5:1–5)

Peter isn't just concerned about his readers entrusting their souls to their faithful Creator. He is also concerned that the elders in the church entrust others' souls to the Chief Shepherd, Jesus Christ. Peter was not only an apostle of Jesus Christ (1:1); he was also an elder, and a fellow elder among those to whom he was writing. He did not place himself above his readers but identified with them as a pastor-shepherd. Peter was more than a fellow elder with his readers though. He had also been a witness to the sufferings of Christ. The gospel of Mark records many examples of Peter witnessing such sufferings, including in the garden of Gethsemane and on the cross of Calvary (Mark 14:32–42; 15:21–39). Peter was also more than a witness of Christ's suffering, however. He was a partaker in the glory that is going to be revealed when Christ comes again. Indeed, he was already partaking of that glory as he followed in the footsteps of his Savior during His life on earth. As those who are in Christ, we share in His glory.

As a shepherd leader, a witness to Christ's suffering, a sufferer himself, and a partaker of Christ's glory, Peter gives his fellow elders a challenging charge. In a culture that would tempt them to lead in all the wrong ways, Peter calls them to lead in the right ways. He uses the imagery of the shepherd interwoven throughout the Old Testament, beginning in Genesis (see Gen. 49:24). Throughout the history of redemption, the Lord used the occupation of shepherds watching over sheep to train His leaders to be shepherds of His people. This was true for Moses as well as for King David (see Ex. 3:1; 1 Sam. 16:11–13). Moreover, leaders in Israel were known as shepherds. Tragically, they were called bad shepherds because they had taken advantage of the sheep and dishonored God's name (see Jer. 23:1–2; Ezek. 34:1–10). In light of these failed shepherds, a brighter light shone through the words of the prophets. Another shepherd would come, a good shepherd who would lead God's people in paths of truth and righteousness (see Ps. 23; Ezek. 34).

The good shepherd motif was fulfilled in Jesus Christ, who is the Chief Shepherd. But the prophets had also prophesied that the Lord would set caring shepherds over His people (Jer. 23:3–4; Ezek. 34:11–31). In His church, He has appointed undershepherds to lead the people of God. But they must lead as Christ Himself led. They must be servant leaders, willing to wash the sheep's feet, getting dirty themselves. As they entrust their souls to the faithful Creator, they must also entrust others' souls to the Chief Shepherd, praying for them and serving them as they lead.

Peter calls the leaders to exercise oversight willingly, because this is God's desire and design for the shepherding ministry. Peter also calls the leaders to exercise oversight eagerly, serving the people regardless of any remuneration. Furthermore, Peter calls the leaders to be examples to the flock, just as Christ had been their example, humbly serving those in their charge. The power- and money-hungry leader has no place in the church of God. Willing, humble, gracious, servant leaders are called to carry the flock, lifting their eyes upward to the Chief Shepherd.

Jesus Himself had not only taught servant leadership by example, washing His disciples' feet (John 13:1–20), but also by exhortation. When James and John requested positions of power and prestige, Jesus corrected them by giving them another idea of the kingdom of God. In Christ's kingdom, suffering, humility, and servanthood are the way forward (see Mark 10:42–45). At the end, far different from earthly glory, the unfading crown of glory awaits those who served as tender shepherds, caring for God's flock in humility and love. Such a crown is ultimately nothing less than Jesus Himself (see Ps. 21:1–7; Isa. 28:5), and the crowns that we do receive will be cast at the feet of our Chief Shepherd, to whom all glory, honor, and power is due (see Rev. 4:10).

Peter's challenging charge to the undershepherds prompts another charge, this time to those who are under the elders' care. We are to be sheep who are a joy to lead and who care for our shepherds as much as they care for us (Heb. 13:17). Peter continues his theme of submission that he began in 2:13. After dealing with several specific situations, he addressed everyone, calling them to unity of mind, sympathy, brotherly love, tenderness, and humility. Now he does so again, addressing the young people in the congregation. But humility crosses all generational boundaries, so he closes by reminding everyone that God opposes the proud and gives grace to the humble, reflecting the wisdom of Proverbs 3:34, which James used as well (see James 4:6, 10). Humility is key for both parties, those who lead and those who follow. Humility is the way of the Lord, and His people are to follow in His footsteps.

These verses remind us of the importance of praying for our pastors and elders on a daily basis. We should pray for their speech and conduct to be godly, their love for the Lord and His people to grow fervent and strong, their faith to be strengthened, and their hearts and minds to be kept pure. These verses also remind us of several key principles for all of us who serve in a shepherding role, whether as a mother to our children at home, as a mentor to the women in our churches, or as a teacher to our covenant children in our churches. We are to willingly, eagerly, and humbly exercise oversight and exhort by example. We must never forget that we are serving under the Chief Shepherd, who loves them and cares for them far better than we ever will or ever can. We must entrust their souls to Him.

### III. Living as Sufferers: Entrusting Our Struggles to the Caring God (5:6–14)

God's mighty hand of deliverance had parted the waters of the Red Sea and stretched over His people, protecting them as they crossed, freeing them from their suffering under the hand of Pharaoh. As mighty as Pharaoh's hand was, God's was far greater. He heard His people's groaning and did something about it. He is the God who cares.

God's mighty hand also delivered Jesus from the power of sin and death by raising Him to new life and exalting Him to God's righteous right hand. God is the one who exalts and brings low. Again, the way of the kingdom is the way of humility. Only as we humble ourselves before Him, acknowledging Him as our Creator and Redeemer, and casting not only our anxieties but also our lives upon Him will he lift us up.

King David knew this as well as any of us. Oppressed by his enemies, his heart was in anguish. Terrifying death knocked at his door. Surprisingly, it wasn't his enemies causing his greatest trouble, but his friend. David took his cry to his Creator and Redeemer. In this context of deep suffering, he was able to comfort others:

> Cast your burden on the LORD,
> And He shall sustain you;
> He shall never permit the righteous to be moved. (Ps. 55:22)

The final and perfect David, Jesus Christ, also exhorted us to cast our cares upon our heavenly Father. He reminds us of our Father's tender care of His creation. If He cares for the birds, how much more will He care for His people? He knows what we need before we even ask Him. As we seek first His kingdom and His righteousness, He takes care of the rest (see Matt. 6:25–34). Jesus also warned us about the choking hazard of the cares of this world. The cares of the world, the deceitfulness of riches, and the desires for other things threaten to choke the word of righteousness out of our hearts and minds, leading to barrenness rather than fruitfulness (see Mark 4:18–19).

It is not just the cares of the world but also Satan who threatens to choke us. God has delivered us from the devouring power of the devil, but that doesn't mean he leaves us alone. He seeks to steal our joy, quench our thirst for spiritual things, and deceive us into thinking power and prestige are better than dependence and humility. We must be sober and vigilant, lest we succumb to his lies, trading truth for deceit. When we recognize the Father of Lies, we must resist him by standing firm in our faith, remembering who we are. We are Christians, following in the footsteps of our suffering Savior. We are also children, part of the family of God, undergoing the same kinds of suffering together.

Such suffering is a gift of grace. Suffering itself is a test to reveal our faith. The same God who has called us to be His chosen children by grace alone is the same God who delivers us from suffering and protects us in the midst of it. Suffering is not the final word. It is a tool in our Redeemer's hand that chisels us into the likeness of His Son. He will restore us, confirm us, strengthen us, and establish us. Such grace should result in worship, as it did for Peter: "To Him be the glory and the dominion forever and ever. Amen" (1 Peter 5:11).

Peter closes his letter by briefly summarizing his reason for writing. In this brief letter, Peter served a hearty dish to strengthen those under his care by declaring the true grace of God and exhorting them to stand firm in it. This is exactly what Jesus had called him to do. After Peter had failed to acknowledge he was a follower of Christ three different times, Jesus restored him on the banks of the Sea of Tiberias by asking three times if he loved Him. With each of Peter's affirmative replies, Jesus answered with an exhortation to feed His sheep (see John 21:15–19).

Peter mentions that he has written by way of Silvanus. It seems likely that Silas (Silvanus) was the bearer of the letter, not the writer of it, but more important to note is that he is Peter's faithful brother. Indeed, Silas had been chosen as one of the leading men among the brothers of the Jerusalem church to deliver a letter to the Gentile believers in Antioch, Syria, and Cilicia. Silas was not only a faithful leader but also a prophet who encouraged the people with many words. During this time Paul chose Silas as his ministry partner for one of his missionary journeys (see Acts 15:22–23, 32, 40). Silas was a ministry partner not just with Paul but also with Timothy, proclaiming Jesus Christ, the Son of God, alongside them (see 2 Cor. 1:19).

One of the reasons Paul chose Silas is because he didn't want to take John Mark, who had earlier deserted Paul and Barnabas and had not continued with them in the work (see Acts 13:13). This caused a disagreement between Barnabas and Paul, which resulted in forming two new missionary teams: Barnabas and John Mark, and Paul and Silas (see Acts 15:36–39). Evidently, John Mark began serving with Peter sometime after he had served with Paul. Just as Timothy was Paul's son in the faith, John Mark was Peter's son in the faith.

It was John Mark's mother who had opened her home to the early church for its meetings and for prayer. Peter had knocked on her door after being miraculously released from prison by an angel of the Lord. He testified to God's mighty hand of deliverance after Rhoda finally let him in (see Acts 12:1–19). John Mark was actually Barnabas's cousin (see Col. 4:10). And although he deserted Paul and Barnabas at one time, he had proven to be useful to Paul in the ministry (see 2 Tim. 4:11).

Peter wrote from Rome and sent greetings from "she who is in Babylon," another way of saying "the church in Rome." Babylon had been replaced by Rome as a world power, but the name *Babylon* had come to stand for whatever world power was threatening to undo God's people at the time. It was a further reminder of the suffering going on among the brotherhood. Peter's readers, who were scattered across Asia Minor, were certainly suffering, but so was the church in Rome.

Peter's final note is one that both exhorts his readers to love one another and extends to his readers peace. Every pastor-shepherd who serves from his own love of the Chief Shepherd desires nothing less than love and peace for his flock. Peter is only able to extend love and peace to his readers because Christ first extended love and peace to him. He knew this from his time alone with the Lord, when Jesus asked him three times if he loved Him. But he also knew the words that Jesus had spoken to the disciples, "Peace I leave with you, My peace I give to you; not as the world gives do I give to you. Let not your heart be troubled, neither let it be afraid" (John 14:27). Peter had known what it was to be afraid to proclaim that he was one of Christ's followers (Mark 14:66–71), and he had experienced a troubled heart when he heard the rooster crow (Mark 14:72). But he also knew the sweet peace that comes from restoration after such denial (see John 21:15–19) and from a willingness to withstand prisons for the sake of Jesus's name (see Acts 5:17–42; 12:1–19). Peter was a pastor-shepherd who had been trained in the school of suffering. He began as a fisherman who thought too highly of himself, but he ended as one who had learned that the way of the Christian is the way of Christ—following in the footsteps of the One who suffered so much for us so that we might be glorified with Him. In Christ alone is our peace and our joy.

Perhaps suffering threatens to undo you today and you would like someone to hold you while you sob, speaking words of truth and hope to you. I want to encourage you to turn to the Chief Shepherd today, the One who knows you by name and cares for you. Entrust your soul to Him, pouring out your heart to Him because He cares for you.

As you walk through the valley with darkness threatening you on every side, He is with you. His rod and His staff will comfort you. He will lead you in paths of righteousness for His name's sake and restore your broken soul. He will extend goodness and mercy to you and will be a constant companion and friend as He carries you through the valley of suffering (see Psalm 23). Trust him, worship Him, and fix your eyes on Him, the Creator and Chief Shepherd of your soul.

# Processing It Together...

1. What do we learn about God in 1 Peter 4:12–5:14?

2. How does this reshape how we should view our present circumstances?

3. What do we learn about God's Son, Jesus Christ?

4. How should this impact our relationship with God and with others?

5. What do we learn about God's covenant with His people?

6. How are we to live in light of this?

7. How can we apply 1 Peter 4:12–5:14 to our lives today and in the future?

8. How should we apply these verses in our churches?

9. Looking back at "Put It in Perspective" in your personal study questions, what did you find challenging or encouraging about this lesson?

10. Looking back at "Principles and Points of Application," how has this lesson impacted your life?

# 2 Peter

## His Divine Power

# Introduction to 2 Peter

The title "The Power of I Am" caught my eye as I flipped through a Christian bookseller's promotional magazine. I was in the middle of studying 2 Peter, and I thought it would make an appropriate subtitle for several reasons. The entire message of 2 Peter centers on remembering three things: (1) the power of God, (2) the power of Christ's coming again confirmed by the prophetic word, and (3) the promise of His coming again.

Sadly, this inspirational author had 2 Peter far from his mind. Instead, the author believed that the words we choose to describe ourselves determine our life's course. He believed that we are able to tap into transformation by affirming our God-given inner strengths, talents, and abilities.

Tragic, isn't it? Instead of exalting the power of God, the author exalted the power of self. Instead of exalting the power of God's word, the author exalted the power of our words. Instead of teaching transformation by God's grace, the author taught transformation by our words. Instead of recognizing the outward means of grace (the Word, the sacraments, and prayer), he focused on the inner means of our own positive thinking.

Peter teaches a different way. He teaches the way of truth in contrast to the way of error. He lifts our eyes off ourselves to "I AM WHO I AM" (Ex. 3:14), pointing us to His power that enables us to live godly lives, the majesty and means of His transformation, and the promise of His coming again.

## The Author, Date, and Audience of 2 Peter

It is beneficial when we study a book of the Bible that we understand what the Scriptures teach us about the human author the Holy Spirit used to speak and write the Word of God (2 Peter 1:21). If you've completed the study of 1 Peter in this book, you already have a good grasp of who Peter was. It would be good, however, as you begin this study of 2 Peter to go back to the introduction to 1 Peter and review the information on pages 3–5 so that the information about the apostle Peter, the date of his writing, and his audience is fresh in your mind.

## The Purpose of 2 Peter

Peter writes as one who knows his time of death is near (1:14). Therefore, these are his last words to his readers. He writes to stir them up to grow in the qualities that accompany saving faith and in the grace and knowledge of Jesus Christ. His letter does not proclaim news that is unknown to his readers but instead serves as a reminder to them of what they already know.

The purpose of 2 Peter becomes even clearer when we take a close look at some key verses in his letter.

- Peter is concerned that his readers both know and grow objectively and experientially in the grace, peace, and knowledge of Jesus Christ (1:2; 3:18).
- Peter reminds believers that God's power has completely equipped us to live godly lives (1:3).
- Peter reminds believers that godly qualities are evidence of saving faith (1:8–9).
- Peter reminds his readers that God's glory and God's word are witnesses against the false teachers that promote man's glory and man's word (1:16–19).
- Peter encourages his readers that the Lord knows how to rescue the godly from trials (2:9a).
- Peter reminds his readers of the day of judgment, during which false teachers will be judged (2:9b).
- Peter reminds his readers that the Lord's patience in fulfilling His promise is due to His desire for people to be saved (3:9, 15).
- Peter warns his readers against ignorance and instability, exhorting them to knowledge and stability in the faith, as well as holiness and godliness (3:11, 17).

## An Outline of 2 Peter

Different and more detailed outlines of 2 Peter can be found in commentaries, but for this Bible study, I suggest the following:

   I.  Remember the Power of God (1:1–15)

  II.  Remember the Powerful Coming of Christ Confirmed by the Prophetic Word (1:16–2:22)

 III. Remember the Promise of His Coming Again (3:1–18)

Each lesson will further divide this broad outline into smaller parts, but for now, note these major divisions in your mind as you prepare to study 2 Peter.

Now that we have reviewed the author, date, and audience of 2 Peter and considered its purpose and outline, let's also review "An Overview of the History of Redemption and Revelation" on pages xvi–xxi and "A Christ-Centered Interpretation of 1 Peter, 2 Peter, and Jude" on pages xxi–xxiii in the introduction to this Bible study. It is important to keep these matters in mind as we take a closer look at 2 Peter.

If you are tempted to believe that the words we choose to describe ourselves determine our life's course and that we are able to tap into transformation by affirming our God-given inner strengths, talents, and abilities, hold that thought. If you are tempted to exalt the power of self rather than the power of God, hold tight. If you are tempted to believe transformation will come by your own words instead of God's word, don't go anywhere. If you are tempted to focus on the inner means of positive thinking instead of the outward means of grace, stop.

Listen to the word of truth through the apostle Peter. Ask the Lord to lift your eyes off yourself and turn them to the "I AM WHO I AM" (Ex. 3:14) and to point you to His power that enables you to live a godly life, the majesty and means of His transformation, and the promise of His coming again.

# Remember
# the Power of God

2 Peter 1:1–15

*Purpose*...

**Head.** What do I need to know from this passage in Scripture?

- God's divine power has granted to me all things that pertain to life and godliness.

**Heart.** How does what I learn from this passage affect my internal relationship with the Lord?

- I am a kingdom disciple who recognizes that God's power enables me to live a godly life.

**Hands.** How does what I learn from this passage translate into action for God's kingdom?

- I will remind others that God's divine power has granted to us all things that pertain to life and godliness.
- I will encourage others to grow in the grace and knowledge of Jesus Christ through the ordinary means of grace.
- I will help others grow in godly qualities by praying for them and discipling them.

# Personal Study...

**Pray.** Ask that God will open up your heart and mind as you study His Word. This is His story of redemption that He has revealed to us, and the Holy Spirit is our teacher.

**Ponder the Passage.** Read 2 Peter in its entirety. Then reread 2 Peter 1:1–15.

- *Point.* What is the point of this passage? How does this relate to the point of the entire book?

- *People.* Who are the main people involved in this passage? What characterizes them?

- *Persons of the Trinity.* Where do you see God the Father, God the Son, and God the Holy Spirit in this passage?

- *Puzzling Parts.* Are there any parts of the passage that you don't quite understand or that seem interesting or confusing?

**Put It in Perspective.**

- *Place in Scripture.* What is the original context of this text? What is the redemptive-historical context—what has or hasn't happened in redemptive history at this point in Scripture? How does this text connect to Christ?

*The following questions will help if you got stuck on any of the previous questions, and they will help you dig a little deeper into the text, putting it all into perspective.*

1. **1:1–2.** (a) If you researched the apostle Peter's background when you were studying 1 Peter, look back at your notes in lesson 1 for a review of what you learned about him then. If not, then using a concordance or another Bible tool, research the Gospels and the book of Acts to gather background information on Peter that will be helpful to know as we work through 2 Peter. What do you learn about him from these books?

   (b) To whom is Peter writing (see also 1 Peter 1:1–2; 2 Peter 3:1)?

(c) Using Scripture, how would you define God's grace and God's peace?

(d) How are grace and peace multiplied to believers?

**2. 1:3–4.** (a) What has God's power given believers? How?

(b) What else has God given believers?

(c) What do believers become partakers of through these promises?

(d) From what do believers escape when they are saved?

**3. 1:5–7.** (a) Peter begins this section with the phrase "but also for this very reason," reminding his readers of something God has already done for them. What has He done for them? What then are they to do?

(b) What are believers to add to their faith?

(c) How do these verses reflect James 2:14–26?

(d) How do believers add these qualities to their faith (see Gal. 5:22–25)?

**4. 1:8–9.** (a) From what do these qualities in believers' lives keep them?

(b) What does a lack of these qualities in believers' lives reveal?

**5. 1:10–11.** (a) How do believers make their calling and election sure (see also Gal. 4:6; 1 John 3:10, 14)?

(b) What is the danger in not practicing the qualities Peter listed in 1:5–7?

(c) What is the reward of those who are truly saved?

**6. 1:12–15.** (a) If Peter's readers already know these qualities and are established in the truth, why is Peter writing them?

(b) How did Jesus make clear to Peter his death (see John 21:18–19)?

(c) How has the church been able to recall Peter's words over the centuries?

**Principles and Points of Application.**

**7. 1:1–2.** (a) What is the encouragement Peter gives you, a believer in the twenty-first century, in verse 1b? Why does this encourage you?

(b) Spend time today thanking the Lord for clothing you in His righteousness.

(c) How are you growing in the knowledge of God and of Jesus our Lord by the means of grace (the Word, the sacraments, and prayer)?

**8. 1:3–4.** (a) We forget that God's power has given us all things that pertain to life and godliness when we forge ahead in our own willpower and strength, give ourselves personal pep talks, and excuse ourselves from living a life of godliness. In what areas of your life do you need to forsake yourself and remember God's power in you?

(b) How do you live your life in light of the truth that God has called us by His own glory and virtue?

(c) Which promises of God found in Scripture have been of specific comfort to you lately, and why?

(d) How does it both encourage and overwhelm you that you have become a partaker of the divine nature? What does this mean? How is it an encouragement to you? Why might it overwhelm you?

(e) In what ways are you still ensnared by lust, or sinful desire? Confess these today, repent of them, and then rest in Christ as you run the race of grace.

**9. 1:5–7.** (a) How are you making every effort to supplement your faith with virtue? Knowledge? Self-control? Perseverance? Godliness? Brotherly kindness? Love?

(b) How are you helping your loved ones to do the same?

**10. 1:8–9.** (a) Are these qualities decreasing, abounding, or staying the same in your life? In order to answer this question, examine your effectiveness and fruitfulness in the knowledge of our Lord Jesus Christ.

(b) In what ways are you tempted each day to forget you were cleansed from your former sins, ending up in blindness and succumbing to sinful desires?

**11. 1:10–11.** (a) In what ways have you been encouraged (with regard to your calling and election) by the presence of these qualities in your life, which are not just qualities that remain in our hearts but manifest themselves through our hands as we reach out to others around us with tangible actions?

(b) How does it encourage you to add these qualities to your faith when you keep the eternal kingdom of our Lord and Savior Jesus Christ in mind?

**12. 1:12–15.** (a) Often believers are guilty of assuming that since they are established in the truth and know what qualities they should have, they don't need to be reminded of them anymore. How does Peter challenge this way of thinking?

(b) Who do you need to lovingly stir up by reminding them of these qualities?

(c) Thank the Lord today for the privilege of owning a Bible and being able to recall what was written down in ages past in the Old and New Testaments.

# Putting It All Together . . .

I am sure that you, like me, have heard a lot about power from the time you were a young child. Different media and toys offer power in the form of superheroes. Education has often boasted power of a different kind. We have been taught that if we achieve and succeed we can be anything we want to be.

The message of power follows us into adulthood as well. Whether it is climbing the corporate ladder or playing the role of supermom, we have been told that we have the power to do amazing things if we set our minds to it and work hard. Most of the time, we are taught that power comes from within. In other words, if we have enough willpower, we can do or be anything or anyone. The problem is this does not prove to be true.

Think of the young girl who was raised to think success was her key to power, position, and prestige. She made the honor roll, she was voted most valuable player on her sports team, and she won all kinds of awards for community service, but by the time she reached college the drive for power almost killed her. She began cutting or starving herself because she realized that power didn't come by grades, sports, or community service after all.

The Bible speaks altogether differently about power than our world does. It speaks not of willpower, but of divine power. And this power is not something that we have to try to tap into or achieve. It has been exercised on our behalf to save us from self-achievement and to call us to God's own glory and excellence. God's power has given to us all things that pertain to life and godliness. We don't have to go and get what we have already gotten. Yet that is so often how we live, even as believers. We search for things or places or people to give us power. It may be as simple as a beverage with caffeine to power us up for the day, or it may be a vacation to give us energy to head into a busy season, or perhaps it is a relationship to bolster our contacts so that we can hopefully get that job we've been eyeing. Whatever it is, we are hoping it will impact our life for the good.

We often try to power up for godliness in the same way. We look for extraordinary measures to give us a "spiritual high" to boost our walk with the Lord. All the while the Lord has offered to us His Word, the sacraments, and prayer to grow us in godliness.

The apostle Peter has much to say about power. Peter, who once thought power could be gained by the sword, had learned that power is granted by God. His message is an important and timely one indeed.

## I. Remember the Power of God: The Grand Exit (1:1–4)

Since you have just finished your study of 1 Peter, you are well acquainted with "Simon Peter, a bondservant and apostle of Jesus Christ" (2 Peter 1:1). As you take up this study of his second letter, however, it would be good for you to review his background by rereading the information in lesson 1 on pages 16–18. Understanding Peter's experiences in the Gospels and the book of Acts, which inform and illuminate his second letter, will bring you to a deeper appreciation for what he says and why he says it. As you review his background, it is important to note that Peter doesn't hold himself up as a super-apostle, but levels all mankind before Christ's righteousness. All those who have been given faith as a free gift are of equal standing. We are robed in the righteousness of Jesus Christ alone. We have nothing to add to promote us above others. We are sinners saved by grace who are now commissioned to point others to the righteous One.

It is only as we come to know the triune God that we know our great need for Him and the overwhelming grace He has displayed to us. As we come to know Him more, we also experience more of His grace and peace in our lives, as He conforms us to His image in knowledge, righteousness, and holiness.

Peter begins by telling believers about God's power. He wants to focus his readers on God's power because the natural tendency of mankind is to focus on our own power. You and I know this well. Too often we have tried to live out a life of godliness by our own strength. Perhaps we think we can be more godly if we follow more rules or if we adhere to the Little Engine That Could's theology of "I think I can, I think I can, I think I can," as if willpower is enough. Peter knows better. He knows that believers need a power outside of themselves to live a life of godliness. Thankfully, he gives us good news. There is not just power, but divine power. God's power has granted believers all things that pertain to life and godliness. This is astounding news! Think about how many times we make excuses about our behavior or give up because knowledge, righteousness, and holiness seem too hard. But here Peter knocks out all those excuses and places truth before our eyes. God's power is the source of our knowledge, righteousness, and holiness.

God has called us to His own glory and excellence. That means we are to image Him, our Creator, as His creation in knowledge, righteousness, and holiness. We know that believers won't do this perfectly on this side of glory because we still sin. But we are being made more like Christ, and it did not keep the author of Hebrews from exhorting believers to "pursue peace with all people, and holiness, without which no one will see the Lord" (Heb. 12:14). Sadly, this is a message sorely lacking in many churches today. The messages of grace without holiness on the one hand, or holiness without grace on the other, seem to have prevailed in the church across the ages. Peter calls us back to the truth that holiness is by grace and is necessary for the believer.

We have not merely been granted all things that pertain to life and godliness; we have also been granted His precious promises. God's promises in Scripture can be summarized in one phrase: I will be your God, and you will be My people (see Ex. 6:7;

Lev. 26:12; Jer. 30:22; 2 Cor. 6:16). Paul tells us that all the promises of God have been fulfilled in Jesus Christ (2 Cor. 1:20). We have actually become partakers of the divine nature because we are in union with Christ. That means we are dead to sin and alive to righteousness (see Rom. 6:1–14). Christ has led us in a second and greater exodus. God's grand exit plan was far greater than deliverance from Egypt. Christ has delivered us from slavery to sin and freed us to live a life of knowledge, righteousness, and holiness. We have escaped the corruption that is in this world because of sinful desire by the eternal promises of God—mainly, to call a people to Himself and preserve them as His people. The grand exit plan was not an end in itself though. It included a grand entrance plan as well.

## II. Remember the Power of God: The Grand Entrance (1:5–15)

Peter makes it clear that what God calls believers to do flows from and is dependent upon what He has already done for believers. God didn't tell Israel to obey His Ten Commandments before He delivered them from Egypt. Instead, God delivered them from Egypt and then told them how they should live as His people. There is a huge difference between the two. Because God has led His people in a grand exit from the corruption in the world because of sinful desire, and because He has given them all things that pertain to life and godliness, He calls them to live out their calling in concrete ways. He is not just concerned with our attitudes but also with our actions that flow from such attitudes. The life of the believer is to be distinct from the unbeliever's. We are to have a different quality of life because we are dealing with a different quantity of power. Indeed, we are dealing with a power of an entirely different kind. We have divine power at work in our lives.

Our effort then to supplement our faith is not in order to achieve salvation—that is a free gift from God. Nor is it in order to reach a higher plane of holiness—we have all obtained a faith of equal standing. Rather, our effort to supplement our faith is to prove how precious and great are the promises of God regarding our salvation. The same God who has the power to save us also has the power to change us. Faith, then, is the foundation on which the other qualities are built, and love is the crowning pinnacle. Those qualities that fall in between are to be seen as one big package with faith and love. We don't pick and choose the qualities we like or those that are easier for us. Instead, we are called to make every effort to display in our lives all the qualities Peter mentions, whether we are at home, at school, at work, or at play. These qualities are grounded in faith, because without faith we wouldn't have God's power, which is necessary for the interweaving of them in our attitudes and actions. They are crowned by love, because without love we wouldn't extend the grace and peace of God to others.

The first quality Peter mentions, faith, refers to our loyalty to God as our Creator and Redeemer. It refers to our commitment to Christ as our Lord and Savior. And it refers to our commitment to walk by the Spirit and not by the flesh. People of faith are faithful to the One who has called them to salvation, extending His grace and peace to them.

Peter's second quality is virtue. The virtuous person goes beyond duty to delight in serving God and others. She does not withdraw from the covenant community but engages it by serving the church with her spiritual gifts. The Proverbs 31 woman is a great example of virtue. She sees service not as a duty but as a delight, and her family and the community praise her because of it.

Third, Peter mentions the quality of knowledge. This is not abstract knowledge, as if cramming our craniums with more information will save us and make us moral. Rather, this refers to the knowledge of God and of Jesus our Lord. As we come to know Jesus in an intimate and affectionate way, we become more and more like Him.

The fourth quality is self-control. As we walk by the Spirit and not by the flesh, we bring all of our appetites under the control of Christ. Though we may want to indulge in the corruption of this world, we yield our desires to the Spirit's control, asking Him to rein in our passions so that we might serve Christ more fruitfully and effectively.

Fifth, Peter mentions steadfastness. It is not easy to bear up under temptation for long periods of time, yet it is necessary. If we are to grow in godliness, we must learn to exhibit Christlike character even in the face of a corrupt world that seems to dangle temptation before our hearts and minds at every opportunity.

Godliness is Peter's sixth quality. We are to remain loyal not only to our King but also to the covenant community around us. This means that our loyalties are no longer to the things of this world, but to the things of the Lord. This means that we will be valiant for the truth, not compromising our faith or leading our brothers and sisters astray.

The seventh quality Peter names is brotherly affection. Believers are to love one another. Our church services are family gatherings. As we are led to worship our heavenly Father by our Elder Brother, Jesus Christ, we are knit together as brothers and sisters in the Lord. We need each other and should love one another in tangible ways.

Finally, Peter mentions love. This is the crowning pinnacle, because love is the greatest quality (see 1 Cor. 13:13). God Himself is love. We love because He first loved us (1 John 4:19). If we do not have love, everything else becomes pointless (1 Cor. 13:1–3). Love must pervade every other quality, and faith must ground them. Virtue without faith and love evolves into mere duty. Knowledge without faith and love creeps toward hardness of heart and mind. Self-control without faith and love swells into pride. Steadfastness without faith and love soars to legalism. Godliness without faith and love gallops toward outward conformity. And brotherly affection without faith and love boasts a lie.

But believers who are immersed and increasing in these qualities will be both effective and fruitful in the knowledge of Christ. It is, after all, the knowledge of Christ that is the foundation of our immersion and increase. Growing in these qualities, then, necessitates that we remember the gospel. We must remember that Christ has lived a life of perfect obedience for us, has borne God's wrath for our sins on the cross, has been raised to new life as the firstfruits of the resurrection, has ascended into heaven where He is now seated at God the Father's righteous right hand, and is coming again soon to save those who are eagerly waiting for Him and judge those who refuse to bow their knee to Him. Practicing these qualities apart from the gospel is mere legalism or moralism, but practicing them in light of the gospel assures us of our calling and election. Indeed, it assures us not only that we have made a grand exit from the corruption of this world, but that we have made a grand entrance into the eternal kingdom of our Lord and Savior Jesus Christ, a kingdom that has already been inaugurated and will be consummated when He comes again.

Peter is not content to move on from the gospel, as so many churches seem to do today, as if there are more important things to teach and preach. Instead, Peter recognizes that we need to be reminded of the gospel every day of our lives, even though we know we are to grow in holiness as part of our salvation and even though we are well-established in the truth. Peter says that he must stir his readers up (1:13). In other words, the temptation is for them to stay idle in their knowledge, letting it slide into the sidelines, instead of growing in their knowledge, letting it soar into the skylines of their lives.

Peter makes it clear to his readers that this letter will likely be his last. Jesus had told him he would die a martyr's death (John 21:18–19). Living in Rome, under the wicked Nero's rule, he likely knew his time was coming to an end. He wasted no words with his readers. At the end of his life, he had something important to say, and, significantly, it wasn't something new. It was a retelling of the old story, the story of Jesus that started in Genesis and climaxed in Christ's life, death, resurrection, and ascension. He told them the entirety of the gospel—Christ set you free from slavery in order to live a life of freedom in which knowledge, righteousness, and holiness should be paramount. Peter's last words were not just for his original readers but also for the church of every age. The gospel is never to be forgotten or marginalized. Since Christ is the climax of the story, He should be preeminent in all of our ministries, from teaching Sunday school to serving on the streets.

Perhaps today power is something you are trying to get instead of something you recognize you have already received. God's divine power has granted to us all things necessary for life and godliness. This is grand news! In a world offering power that consistently falters and disappoints us, it is a glorious thought to know that God's power has given us what is necessary for us to live for His glory. Far from being called to live for our own glory and excellence by our own power, God has called us to His glory and excellence, exercising His divine power on our behalf.

# Processing It Together...

1. What do we learn about God in 2 Peter 1:1–15?

2. How does this reshape how we should view our present circumstances?

3. What do we learn about God's Son, Jesus Christ?

4. How should this impact our relationship with God and with others?

5. What do we learn about God's covenant with His people?

6. How are we to live in light of this?

7. How can we apply 2 Peter 1:1–15 to our lives today and in the future?

8. How should we apply these verses in our churches?

9. Looking back at "Put It in Perspective" in your personal study questions, what did you find challenging or encouraging about this lesson?

10. Looking back at "Principles and Points of Application," how has this lesson impacted your life?

# Remember the Powerful Coming of Christ

2 Peter 1:16–2:22

*Purpose* . . .

**Head.** What do I need to know from this passage in Scripture?

- The powerful coming of Christ is confirmed by the prophetic word; He will come again in honor and glory to put an end to heresy and godlessness.

**Heart.** How does what I learn from this passage affect my internal relationship with the Lord?

- I am a kingdom disciple who reflects the honor and glory of the Lord.

**Hands.** How does what I learn from this passage translate into action for God's kingdom?

- I will help others dissolve devised myths and embrace truth instead.
- I will help others prioritize the study of God's Word.
- I will pray for the purity of the church of Christ.
- I will pray for those I know living ungodly lives.
- I will help others grow in their faith by praying for them and pointing them to the means of grace (the Word, the sacraments, and prayer).
- I will expose the lure of false freedom and point others to true freedom in Christ.

# Personal Study...

**Pray.** Ask that God will open up your heart and mind as you study His Word. This is His story of redemption that He has revealed to us, and the Holy Spirit is our teacher.

**Ponder the Passage.** Read 2 Peter 1:16–2:22.

- *Point.* What is the point of this passage? How does this relate to the point of the entire book?

- *People.* Who are the main people involved in this passage? What characterizes them?

- *Persons of the Trinity.* Where do you see God the Father, God the Son, and God the Holy Spirit in this passage?

- *Puzzling Parts.* Are there any parts of the passage that you don't quite understand or that seem interesting or confusing?

**Put It in Perspective.**

- *Place in Scripture.* Since you have studied 2 Peter's place in Scripture in lesson 6, you may want to take this opportunity to review your answer.

*The following questions will help if you got stuck on any of the previous questions, and they will help you dig a little deeper into the text, putting it all into perspective.*

1. **1:16–18.** (a) In verse 16, what does Peter say he has made known to his readers? What contrasts with that message?

(b) How does this anticipate the subject Peter will take up in chapter 2?

(c) For background on these verses, read the account of the transfiguration in Matthew 17:1–13; Mark 9:2–13; and Luke 9:28–36.

(d) Read Psalm 2:6–7 and Isaiah 42:1, which both point forward to Christ. What roles does He have in these verses? How is Peter recalling these two passages in verse 17?

**2. 1:19–21.** (a) The first witness of Christ's powerful coming that Peter discusses is the transfiguration. What is the second witness he mentions?

(b) What simile does Peter use to describe the prophetic word (see also Ps. 119:105; John 5:30–47)?

(c) To what does the phrase "until the day dawns" refer (see 2 Peter 3:4, 7, 10, 12–13)?

(d) To whom does "morning star" refer (see Num. 24:16; Rev. 22:16)?

(e) What reasons does Peter give to confirm that we should pay attention to the prophetic word (see also 2 Tim. 3:16; 1 Peter 1:10–12)?

**3. 2:1–3.** (a) What does the Old Testament teach us about false prophets (see Deut. 18:20–22; Jer. 14:13–15; 23:16–32; 27:16–18; Ezek. 13:1–23; Mic. 3:5–12)?

(b) What did Jesus have to say about false prophets (see Matt. 7:15–20; 24:3–28)?

(c) For Peter, who were the contemporary "false prophets"?

(d) How do the false teachers bring in destructive heresies?

(e) What does Peter give as an example of their destructive heresies?

(f) What do the false teachers bring upon themselves?

(g) What number of people will follow the false teachers, and what specifically will they follow?

(h) How will the false teachers impact the way of truth?

(i) What is the motivation of their exploitation with false words?

(j) What is neither idle nor asleep for the false teachers?

**4. 2:4–10a.** (a) What three examples from the Old Testament does Peter use to confirm that the Lord will judge the ungodly?

(b) For background on these Old Testament examples, read Genesis 6:1–4; 6:5–7:24; and 18:16–19:29. What do you learn?

(c) What two examples from the Old Testament does Peter use to confirm that the Lord will save the godly?

(d) For background on these Old Testament examples, read Genesis 6:8–9:17 and 19:1–29.

(e) How does Peter use these five examples to both encourage and warn his readers (see also Luke 17:22–37)?

(f) How do verses 9b–10a characterize the sin of the false teachers in their midst, as well as their judgment?

(g) What does Jesus have to say about people who confess Him with their lips and deny Him with their lifestyles (see Matt. 7:21–23)?

**5. 2:10b–16.** (a) How does Peter contrast the false teachers with the good angels?

(b) How are false teachers like animals?

(c) What will be the false teachers' end?

(d) How do the false teachers interact with the Christian community?

(e) How does Peter describe their eyes and hearts (see also Matt. 5:27–30)?

(f) How does Peter use the example of Balaam to illustrate the way of the false teachers (for background on Balaam, read Num. 22:1–25:9; 31:9, 16)?

**6. 2:17–22.** (a) What metaphors does Peter use to describe the false teachers? Contrast these with what you learn about Jesus in John 4:13–14; 7:37–39; and Revelation 22:17.

(b) What is reserved for them?

(c) How are they alluring, or enticing, others?

(d) What kind of people are targets for their evangelism?

(e) Why can the false teachers never fulfill their promise of freedom (see John 8:31–38)?

(f) Why is it worse to forsake Christian teaching than to never have embraced it in the first place (see Matt. 12:43–45 and Heb. 6:4–6)?

(g) What two proverbs does Peter use to confirm his claim (see also Prov. 26:11)?

(h) How did the Jews view dogs and pigs (see Lev. 11:7; Matt. 7:6; Rev. 22:15)?

**Principles and Points of Application.**

**7. 1:16–18.** (a) How often are your thoughts turned toward the majesty of God, the powerful coming of our Lord and Savior Jesus Christ, and the honor and glory that is due Him? What can you do that will help you turn your thoughts to these things more frequently?

(b) Spend time worshiping Him right now.

(c) What "cunningly devised fables" have you been tempted to believe?

**8. 1:19–21.** (a) How can you make reading and studying the Word of God a priority in your daily life?

(b) What instruction in these verses shows why the Word of God should have priority in your daily life?

**9. 2:1–3.** (a) Name some destructive heresies that are circulating in churches today.

(b) How has sensuality in the church today cast a shadow on the way of truth?

(c) How has greed caused many men to fall in the church today?

(d) Spend time in prayer for the church today, specifically for your local church. Pray that the Lord will purify your congregation, that truth will be upheld, that Christ will be preeminent, and that the love of money would be replaced with the love of giving.

**10. 2:4–10a.** (a) What is your reaction to the worldliness that you observe?

(b) As a godly person, what encouragement do you receive from these verses?

(c) Spend time in prayer for those you know who are living ungodly lifestyles. Pray that the Lord will save their souls and free them from the lust of passion and lack of submission to authority.

**11. 2:10b–16.** (a) Do you consider yourself an "unstable soul"? Why or why not?

(b) In what ways do you need to grow in steadfastness regarding the faith?

(c) Ask the Lord to give you eyes full of purity and a heart trained in godliness.

(d) In what ways are you tempted to love gain?

**12. 2:17–22.** (a) To what are you enslaved (alcohol, beauty, career, diet and exercise, food, gaming, leisure, media, money, power, prestige, position, sexual sin, shopping, or video games)?

(b) Read John 8:31–38. True freedom is found only in Christ. Ask the Lord to set you free from false masters.

(c) Pray today for the people you know who have once known the way of righteousness and have turned away from it to indulge in the way of worldliness again.

## Putting It All Together…

We are living in a day when many people have lost appreciation for the majesty of God and His Word. This has had dire consequences. Some Christians have traded in a God-centered theology for a man-centered one. They have exchanged the Bible for the books of men. They have exalted heroes of the faith more than the Hero of the faith, Jesus Christ. They have exchanged God's promises and freedom for man's promises and enslavement. And they have forgotten the doctrines of grace, thinking they are pretty good people who can earn God's favor, that there are many ways to heaven, that God's grace is license to sin, and that people are capable of preserving their destinies.

Peter puts our gaze back where it belongs. In this part of his letter, he points us to the majesty of Christ and His Word. By denouncing the false teachers of his day, he reminds us that if we remove our gaze from these two witnesses, we are in deep danger. Christ and Scripture anchor us in the midst of a plethora of wells without water offered by our culture today.

In the previous portion of his letter, Peter exhorted his readers to remember the power of God. We looked at two important truths regarding God's power. First, a grand exit—believers have escaped from the corruption that is in the world because of sinful desire (2 Peter 1:4). Second, a grand entrance—believers have been richly provided an entrance into the eternal kingdom of our Lord and Savior Jesus Christ (2 Peter 1:11). Now, Peter moves on in this portion of his letter (1:16–2:22) to exhort us to remember the powerful coming of Christ confirmed by the prophetic word. Again, we will look at two important truths concerning this topic. First, we will look at the honor and glory of Christ; second, we will look at the heresy and godlessness of false teachers.

### I. Remember the Powerful Coming of Christ Confirmed by the Prophetic Word: Honor and Glory (1:16–21)

The apostle Peter, previously a fisherman who had fished for true hope all his life and never caught it, had now been hooked by his Master, Jesus Christ, and had been given true hope, grace, and peace. He was called to follow Him and had been exhorted to feed the other sheep of Christ's flock. Peter had indeed seen the majesty of his Master.

Jesus had taken Peter, James, and John up a high mountain so that they could witness His transfiguration. Peter learned some important lessons on that mountain that would inform his future worship, work, and witness for the kingdom. First, he learned that God would not share the worship of His Son with anyone else (Matt. 17:1–5). When Moses and Elijah appeared and began talking with Jesus, Peter wanted to make a tent for each of them. But God the Father replied, "This is My beloved Son, in whom I am well pleased. Hear Him!" (Matt. 17:5). Second, Peter learned that he did not have to stand before God in fear (Matt. 17:6–8). When Peter heard God the Father's voice, he was terrified. But Jesus touched him and told him not to have any fear and to rise to his feet. Peter learned that apart from Jesus we would not be able to stand in the terrifying presence of God the Father, but with Jesus, we do not have anything to fear. All those who are in Christ can come before the Father with no fear because Christ has both lived for us and died for us. We are clothed in His righteousness and covered by His atoning blood. Third, he learned that Jesus would suffer at the hands of men, even unto death; would be raised from the dead; and would restore all things as the greatest and final Moses and Elijah (Matt. 17:9–13).

Peter recalls this experience on the mountain with his Master as he pens his second letter. In anticipation of his long refute of false teachers in chapter 2, he explains to his readers that he "did not follow cunningly devised fables"; rather, he defends the truth that he follows the One who received honor and glory from God the Father, the conferral of which he was privileged to witness on the holy mountain. The transfiguration was not the consummation of such conferral, which will be at Christ's second and final coming, but it was the inauguration of Christ's exalted status as the honored and glorious Son of God, which had been confirmed at His baptism as well (see Luke 3:21–22).

God the Father's words to His Son recall two important passages from the Old Testament. First, Psalm 2, which speaks of the Lord and His anointed, is the backdrop for His words. The psalm points forward to Jesus Christ, the King who has been set on Zion, God's holy hill, as the ruler of the nations. The Lord God confers the title of Son on His chosen King and proclaims that the nations will be His inheritance and the earth His possession. Then the psalmist exhorts his readers to serve the Lord with fear, to rejoice with trembling, and to take refuge in Him. Second, Isaiah 42, which is the first of the Servant Songs in the book, serves as the backdrop for the Father's words to His Son, specifically verse 1:

> Behold! My servant whom I uphold,
> My Elect One in whom My soul delights!

I have put My Spirit upon Him;
He will bring forth justice to the Gentiles.

Peter's use of these two passages juxtaposes Jesus's role as the King who comes to extend peace and mercy and His role as the Suffering Servant who comes to live and die for us so that we can have peace and mercy. He is both the Lord of the covenant and the Servant of the covenant, the Lord of Israel and the servant Israel. He is indeed the one who will powerfully come again to save those who are eagerly waiting for Him and to judge those who refuse to bow their knee to Him.

Peter transitions from writing about one witness of Christ's powerful coming—the transfiguration—to a second witness—the prophetic word (1:19–21). Christ's first coming was certainly a miraculous and majestic event, but it was not unexpected. Jesus Himself proclaimed that He was the fulfillment of all things written about Him in the Law of Moses, the Prophets, and the Psalms (see Luke 24:25–27, 44–47). Peter had the privilege of seeing the light of Christ's glory on the holy mountain, but he wanted his readers to know that they had the privilege of the light of Scripture. It was not just their privilege but also their duty to pay attention to such a gift. After all, this is not a gift from man, nor is it man's idea. Scripture is a gift from God, and it is His idea. The Holy Spirit of God used humans to pen Scripture, but it was God's word that they wrote, not their own. To be sure, He used their experiences, their personalities, and their passions as He produced the different books of Scripture, but He is the ultimate author. God's Word is a gift to His people to be enjoyed until the day Christ (the Morning Star) comes again or until the day we are called home to glory. It is a means of grace that He uses to both comfort us and conform us to the image of His Son. Christ's Spirit transforms our hearts as we reflect on the Christ of the Word.

Paying attention to God's word is much more than a casual reading of Scripture every now and then. It is making every effort to place ourselves under the preaching of God's Word in a Bible-believing church each Sunday and reading, studying, and meditating upon Scripture on our own during the week. It is praying that the Lord will prepare our hearts, minds, and ears as we listen so that His word will effect life change in us. Our study of God's Word should leave us singing a song with the psalmist:

Oh, how I love Your law!
It is my meditation all the day….
How sweet are Your words to my taste,
Sweeter than honey to my mouth!…
Your word is a lamp to my feet
And a light to my path. (Ps. 119:97, 103, 105)

123

## II. Remember the Powerful Coming of Christ Confirmed by the Prophetic Word: Heresy and Godlessness (2:1–22)

Peter reminds his readers that in contrast to the good prophets who spoke from God (2 Peter 1:21), during the same time there were false prophets who spoke from their own perverse wills. The Lord told Israel that He would raise up prophets to speak His words, the ultimate fulfillment of which comes in the final prophet, Jesus Christ. At the same time He told them there would be prophets who presumed to speak with His authority, but these were false prophets who were speaking their own words, the punishment of which would be death (Deut. 18:20–22). Several prophets spoke against the false prophets who arose in Israel, charging them with deceitful ways and with leading Israel astray by their lies and recklessness, as well as practicing divination for money (see Deut. 18:20–22; Jer. 14:13–15; 23:16–32; 27:16–18; Ezek. 13:1–23; Mic. 3:5–12).

Jesus, the final and greatest prophet, had something to say about false prophets as well. He warned His disciples of them, because they are not recognized by their outward appearance but by their outward actions that flow from a heart filled with bad fruit (see Matt. 7:15–20). Jesus told them that these false prophets would lead many people astray, especially near the time of His second coming. Lawlessness would increase, and love would decrease (see Matt. 24:3–28).

Peter warns his readers that just as there were false prophets in the past, there are false teachers in the present. They grow from the same bad root and produce bad fruit. Their methods are manipulative, as they secretly introduce errors. Their message is heretical, even a denial of the Master, Jesus Christ. Such manipulative methods and mythical messages would be met with swift destruction. The Lord will not allow the ungodly to flourish but will judge them for their false teaching.

Their motives were as bad as their manipulative methods and mythical messages. First, they were motivated by sensuality, justifying the way of falsehood instead of truth. Second, they were motivated by greed, exploiting the believers with false words. Such malevolent motives would not be overlooked. The Lord who is judge of all the earth will not stand aside forever. Their condemnation and destruction will not be an afterthought but has been known from long ago. The time of judgment is growing riper as the revilers run headlong into repulsive error.

Peter's purpose is not just to warn his readers about false teachers in their midst. He also wants to encourage his readers. Thus, in proving that the false teachers' condemnation is not idle and their destruction is not asleep (2:3), he confirms that the Lord will judge the ungodly, and, at the same time, he comforts them with the truth that the Lord will rescue the godly (2:9–10).

He confirms the false teachers' condemnation by using three Old Testament examples. First, Peter mentions rebellious angels. This story is based on a Jewish interpretation of Genesis 6:1–4 which claims that angels mated with humans and produced giants. Peter's point is not what happened, but what resulted. God committed them to future judgment. So too were the false teachers committed to future judgment.

Second, Peter points out that God brought a flood upon the ungodly in Noah's day (see Gen. 6:5–7:24). Just as God did not spare the ungodly then, neither would He spare the ungodly now. Third, Peter references the sin-filled cities of Sodom and Gomorrah, both of which were burned up with the fire of judgment (see Gen. 18:16–19:29). Just as God condemned these sinful cities to destruction, so too He had already condemned the false teachers to destruction.

At the same time Peter confirms the false teachers' destruction, he also comforts the godly by highlighting two righteous men who lived during the days of the flood and the days of Sodom and Gomorrah—Noah and Lot. First, God preserved righteous Noah and his family in the midst of judging the ungodly (see Gen. 6:8–9:17). Second, He rescued righteous Lot in the midst of judging the sensual cities of Sodom and Gomorrah (see Gen. 19:1–29). The trials these two men endured were great. Noah proclaimed the way of righteousness to a perverse world that did not listen, and Lot lived righteously in the midst of mankind rebelling against God's authority. But even in this great degradation, the gracious Lord delivered Noah and Lot. They were not swept away with those who indulged in the lust of defiling passion and despised authority but were rescued by the Redeemer. So too the Lord could rescue Peter's readers from the snare of the false teachers, saving their souls from the false teachers' malevolent motives, manipulative methods, and mythical messages.

Peter wasn't the first to refer to the flood and Sodom in relation to God's judgment. Jesus Himself had taught Peter (and the other disciples) about the final day of judgment by using the ancient flood and Sodom as an illustration. Just as the world was carrying on without one look at their Creator and Redeemer when judgment came upon them in the form of the flood and fire and brimstone, so too the world will be carrying on without one look at their Creator and Redeemer when the Son of Man comes again. Those who are seeking to preserve their life through the things of this world will lose it, but those who have given their life up to Christ will be privileged to experience eternal life with Him.

Peter illustrates how the false teachers despise authority by contrasting them with the good angels. The false teachers are bold and willful, blaspheming the angels who were appointed as God's messengers and given might and power. Yet the angels withhold pronouncing a blaspheming judgment against the false teachers, submitting to the Lord as judge. In contrast to the false teachers, the good angels know their place, remaining humble and submitted to God's will. Peter says that the false teachers are driven by irrationality, instinct, and ignorance, which will end in destruction. The wages of wrongdoing is suffering wrong.

The false teachers are so swept away by sensuality that they even revel in the daytime. But what is worse is that they revel in their deceptions while feasting with the covenant community, and the purpose of the feast was to celebrate the Lord's Supper. In the midst of the church that Christ is making to be without spot and blemish (see Eph. 5:27), the revelers are spots and blemishes, staining the feast with the sensuality of the world. They blinked adulterous eyes that could never be satisfied by sensual sin and beat greedy hearts that could never be gratified by gain. They enticed those who were not strong in the faith to go astray from the right way with them, following the way of Balaam.

By Peter's day the way of Balaam had become proverbial for the way of wrong-doing. The story of Balaam is recorded in the book of Numbers (see Num. 22:1–25:9; 31:9, 16). The king of Balak summoned this prophet to curse the nation of Israel, but the Lord would not allow His blessed people to be cursed. Like the false teachers, Balaam loved gain from wrongdoing and was driven by irrationality, instinct, and igno-rance. In an ironic twist, his own donkey (which naturally would have been driven by irrationality, instinct, and ignorance) spoke to him with rationality and reason in order to restrain Balaam's madness. There is another connection between Balaam and the false prophets. They both loved the lust of defiling passion. Balaam advised Israel to whore with the daughters of Moab in idolatrous and immoral worship of Moab's gods, which they did. The result was a plague of judgment that killed twenty-four thousand Israelites (see Num. 25:1–9; 31:16). The false teachers would certainly be judged for their idolatry and immorality as well.

Peter continues to expose the false teachers' malevolent motives, manipulative methods, and mythical messages (2:17–22). He uses two metaphors to describe them—"wells without water" and "clouds carried by a tempest" (v. 17). Wells without water offer no refreshment for the thirsty. So too the false teachers offer no spiritual refreshment for those who are spiritually thirsty. Clouds carried by a tempest fail to offer refreshing rains; instead, they produce a faint mist prior to a storm, offering no satisfaction to a parched ground. So too the false teachers offer no spiritual satisfaction to those who are parched spiritually. Instead of having a seat reserved at the table of the Lamb, they have an eternal reservation with the gloom of darkness.

In contrast, Jesus (the greatest and truest teacher of all) offers water that will quench our thirst forever. The water Jesus offers becomes a spring of water welling up to eternal life (John 4:13–14). Jesus, speaking of the Holy Spirit, promised that rivers of living water would flow from believers' hearts (John 7:37–39).

Peter continues to describe the false teachers' manipulative methods (2:18–19). They speak loudly, grabbing the attention of others, and boast in folly instead of truth. They target those who are new to the way of truth, enticing them by sensual passions of the flesh. They promise them a freedom that they don't even have themselves. In fact, they are slaves to their own sensuality—a slavery they can't even see because they have sunk so deeply in sinfulness.

In contrast to the false teachers, Jesus offers true freedom. When Jesus was speak-ing to the Jews who had believed in Him, he told them that "whoever commits sin is a slave of sin," but "if the Son makes you free, you shall be free indeed" (John 8:34, 36). Jesus died to set us free from slavery to sin so that we could be free to serve Him. He frees us from the hard yoke and heavy burden of life without Christ, replacing it with an easy yoke and a light burden (see Matt. 11:28–30).

Peter closes his denunciation of the false prophets' malevolent motives, manipulative methods, and mythical messages with a sobering declaration (2:20–22). Peter says that it would have been better for the false teachers to have never known the way of righteousness than to know it and turn away from it to the way of wickedness. They had escaped the defilements of the world through the knowledge of Christ and dove headlong into them again. When a person turns away from the only One who can deliver her from perversion, her last state is worse than the first because she has given up the only way of true freedom (see also Heb. 6:4–6). Peter alludes to two proverbs to solidify his point, one of which is found in Proverbs 26:11, "As a dog returns to his own vomit, so a fool repeats his folly." Like unclean dogs and pigs, both of which Israel was to have nothing to do with, the false teachers are unclean, and the covenant community is to have nothing to do with their ways. They have returned to their own folly, forsaking freedom offered in Christ for the false, futile, and fleeting freedom offered by the world.

Where is your gaze today? Are you fixated on the majesty of Christ and of His word? Do you believe that Christ and Scripture anchor us in the midst of wells without water? If you don't, you are in danger of trading in a God-centered theology for a man-centered one; of exchanging the Bible for the books of man; of exalting heroes of the faith more than the Hero of the faith, Jesus Christ; of exchanging God's promises and freedom for man's promises and enslavement; and of forgetting the doctrines of grace, thinking you are a pretty good person who can earn God's favor, that there are many ways to heaven, that God's grace is license to sin, and that you are capable of preserving your destiny. Let us fix our eyes on our Redeemer, eagerly awaiting His powerful coming, which is confirmed by the prophetic word.

# Processing It Together...

1. What do we learn about God in 2 Peter 1:16–2:22?

2. How does this reshape how we should view our present circumstances?

3. What do we learn about God's Son, Jesus Christ?

4. How should this impact our relationship with God and with others?

5. What do we learn about God's covenant with His people?

6. How are we to live in light of this?

7. How can we apply 2 Peter 1:16–2:22 to our lives today and in the future?

8. How should we apply these verses in our churches?

9. Looking back at "Put It in Perspective" in your personal study questions, what did you find challenging or encouraging about this lesson?

10. Looking back at "Principles and Points of Application," how has this lesson impacted your life?

# Remember the Promise
# of His Coming Again

2 Peter 3:1–18

## Purpose...

**Head.** What do I need to know from this passage in Scripture?

- Christ's second coming must be viewed in light of the word of God, the patience of God, the salvation of God, and the glory of God.

**Heart.** How does what I learn from this passage affect my internal relationship with the Lord?

- I am a kingdom disciple who waits for and hastens the coming day of God while living a life of holiness and godliness.

**Hands.** How does what I learn from this passage translate into action for God's kingdom?

- I will respond to scoffers of the faith with truth.
- I will reflect God's patience and desire for people to come to repentance in my interactions with unbelievers.
- I will help others keep an eternal perspective in the midst of the mundane.
- I will lovingly exhort others to grow in holiness and godliness.
- I will grow in the grace and knowledge of Jesus Christ in the context of the covenant community.

# Personal Study...

**Pray.** Ask that God will open up your heart and mind as you study His Word. This is His story of redemption that He has revealed to us, and the Holy Spirit is our teacher.

**Ponder the Passage.** Read 2 Peter 3:1–18.

- *Point.* What is the point of this passage? How does this relate to the point of the entire book?

- *People.* Who are the main people involved in this passage? What characterizes them?

- *Persons of the Trinity.* Where do you see God the Father, God the Son, and God the Holy Spirit in this passage?

- *Puzzling Parts.* Are there any parts of the passage that you don't quite understand or that seem interesting or confusing?

**Put It in Perspective.**

- *Place in Scripture.* Since you have studied 2 Peter's place in Scripture in lesson 6, you may want to take this opportunity to review your answer.

*The following questions will help if you got stuck on any of the previous questions, and they will help you dig a little deeper into the text, putting it all into perspective.*

**1. 3:1–7.** (a) How does Peter address his readers?

(b) How does Peter desire to stir up his readers' minds? What does he want them to remember?

(c) What is Peter's primary concern in his second letter?

(d) What do the scoffers question, and why?

(e) What fact do they willfully forget?

(f) For background on creation and the flood, read Genesis 1:1–31 and 6:1–9:17.

(g) How does Peter relate the word of God to both creation and judgment?

(h) For what does Peter tell us the present heavens and earth are stored up?

(i) What imagery does the Old Testament use for judgment (see Isa. 29:6; 30:27–33; 33:14; 66:15–16; Joel 2:30; Nah. 1:6; Zeph. 1:18; 3:8; Mal. 4:1)?

(j) How does Peter reflect Jesus's teaching of the last days (see Matt. 11:20–24; 12:33–37, 41–42; 13:24–30, 36–43, 47–50; 24:1–25:46)?

**2. 3:8–10.** (a) Compare Peter's wording about the false teachers in 3:5a with his exhortation to believers.

(b) How is the Lord's time different from our time?

(c) Read Psalm 90, and record the context, especially of Psalm 90:4.

(d) How does Peter explain the Lord's seeming slowness in fulfilling His promise (see also Ex. 34:6; Joel 2:13; Jonah 4:2; Hab. 2:3)?

(e) How does Peter describe the coming day of the Lord (see also Isa. 34:4; 51:6; Matt. 24:43–44)?

**3. 3:11–13.** (a) How should we live in light of the coming day of God?

(b) How does Peter reiterate in these verses what he has already spoken of in 3:8–10?

(c) On what is our hope for new heavens and a new earth in which righteousness dwell founded?

(d) What similarities are there between these verses and Isaiah 65:17 and 66:22?

**4. 3:14–16.** (a) As we wait for new heavens and a new earth, in what are we to be diligent?

(b) How does "without spot and blameless" contrast with the false teachers (see 2 Peter 2:13)?

(c) Who makes us to be "without spot and blameless" (see Eph. 5:25–27; 1 Peter 1:19)?

(d) Only as people are at peace with God can they be at peace with one another. How do we have peace with God (see Rom. 5:1)?

(e) How are we to view the longsuffering of the Lord?

(f) How does Peter refer to Paul?

(g) About what do Paul and Peter both write?

(h) How have the ignorant and unstable handled Paul's writings, as well as other passages of Scripture?

**5. 3:17–18.** (a) How do the ignorance and instability of the false teachers serve as a warning for believers?

(b) What does Peter suggest as the solution to straying from the stability of the faith?

(c) How does Peter's exaltation of Christ in the present, as well as in the future, continue to secure his argument against the beliefs of the false teachers?

**Principles and Points of Application.**

**6. 3:1–7.** (a) What things has Peter written about in this second letter that have emphasized how important it is that you remember the truth?

(b) In what ways have you encountered scoffers who follow their own sinful desires (for example, in Christian media, literature, or teaching)?

(c) What passages from the Word of God have helped you respond to such messages?

**7. 3:8–10.** (a) How does the reason for God's delay of returning to judge the living and the dead encourage you?

(b) How do you reflect His patience and desire in your interactions with others, especially unbelievers (see 2 Cor. 6:6; Gal. 5:22; Eph. 4:2; Col. 1:11; 3:12; 1 Tim. 3:10; 4:2; Heb. 6:12)?

(c) In what ways do you live in light of eternity each day, even in the midst of the mundane?

(d) How does keeping an eternal perspective change the way you live in the present?

**8. 3:11–13.** (a) What areas of your life reflect holiness and godliness?

(b) In what areas of your life do you need to grow in holiness and godliness?

(c) Spend time in prayer asking the Lord to help you grow in holiness and godliness in specific areas as well as live everyday life in light of eternity.

**9. 3:14–16.** (a) How are you being diligent to be found by the Lord without spot and blameless and at peace?

(b) How are you counting the longsuffering of our Lord as salvation?

(c) How have you seen ignorance and instability lead to immorality in your own life or in the lives of your loved ones?

**10. 3:17–18.** (a) What practices in your life must you prioritize so that you remain stable in the faith?

(b) Earlier in his letter, Peter exhorted believers to grow in several qualities (1:5–8), but now he exhorts them to grow in the grace and knowledge of Jesus Christ. Such growth is recognizing the power of the gospel to transform our lives into God's image and intimately knowing Jesus Christ. How is God's grace not only saving you but also sanctifying you, making you more and more holy and godly? Do you love Jesus as Lord and Savior of your life?

## Putting It All Together...

I have a hard time being patient. When I strongly desire that something happen in my life, I have a difficult time waiting to see whether or not it is the Lord's time to bring it to pass. Looking back over the years of my life, there are several significant events for which I had a hard time waiting. It was hard to wait to see if I made the basketball team in high school. It was difficult for me to wait for college acceptance letters. It was hard to wait for graduation from seminary and the securing of a ministry position. It was difficult to wait for marriage. It was hard to wait to get pregnant. It was difficult to wait for my first publication, as well as subsequent ones. It has also been hard to wait for the Lord to complete the good work He has begun in me as well as in my loved ones (which won't be until glory!). And it has been difficult to wait for answered prayers regarding loved ones who are not saved.

In each time of waiting, I have been tempted to exchange the true riches of the eternal for the false riches of the temporal. I have wanted to run ahead of the Lord's timing in order to secure my desired outcome on my own. I have been tempted to think that the Lord has forgotten His promise to work all things out in my life for my good and His glory. I have been tempted to overlook the fact that the Lord has His own timetable, and it is not mine. I have been tempted to think that I love my loved ones and desire their salvation more than the Lord does. I have been tempted to think that my ways are better than His. And I have been tempted to secure my own glory instead of giving glory to Him.

I regret how I waited in many of my circumstances. Instead of worshiping God, I often wrestled with Him. Rather than accepting His plan, I often tried to alter it. Instead of inviting Him to be Lord over my situation, I often invented ways to try to accomplish what I wanted on my own. And instead of trusting His ways, I often trumpeted my own.

Peter gives an important word to someone like me, and I imagine someone like you too. He reminds us of the importance of waiting for God's promises, of recognizing that His timetable is different from ours, and of growing in the grace and knowledge of Jesus Christ. He warns us against ignorance and instability, both of which so easily entrap us, and exhorts us to be diligent in standing firm in the faith.

## I. Remember the Promise of His Coming Again: The Word of God (3:1–7)

Peter writes as a shepherd of the sheep for the Chief Shepherd of the sheep. In both his letters, Peter has tried hard to stir up the believers' minds to remember the word of God (see 1 Peter 1:10–12, 25; 2:6–8; 3:10–12) and to remember His coming (see 1 Peter 1:3–7; 2:12; 4:7; 5:4, 10). Specifically in his second letter, he has reminded his readers that not only the prophets but also the Lord Himself had predicted that scoffers with sinful desires would come in the last days, questioning the promise of Christ's return. They would mistakenly assume that God had not interrupted history since the time of creation, but they were wrong. They deliberately overlooked truth to continue in their deluge of lies.

First, they deliberately overlooked God as Creator. He had created the world by His word. Second, they deliberately overlooked God as judge. He had judged the world of Noah's day with a flood, sparing only Noah and his family by way of an ark. In the same way, He would judge the scoffers of Peter's day on the final day of judgment. Finally, they deliberately overlooked God's providence and sovereignty. They were blinded to the truth that the same word of God that created the world also upholds the world. Redemptive history is marching forward to the day when Christ will come to judge the living and the dead. The ungodly will meet their Maker on that day, and they will be judged for refusing to acknowledge Him as Creator, judge, and sovereign over all.

Peter's imagery of fire for judgment is not new. The Old Testament prophets had spoken of the day of judgment with the imagery of fire as well (see Isa. 29:6; 30:27–33;

33:14; 66:15–16; Joel 2:30; Nah. 1:6; Zeph. 1:18; 3:8; Mal. 4:1). More importantly, Jesus, the greatest and final prophet, continued to speak of the day of judgment with the imagery of fire (see Matt. 11:20–24; 12:33–37, 41–42; 13:24–30, 36–43, 47–50; 24:1–25:46). Peter had learned at the feet of Jesus and was now warning his readers that the scoffers of their day would be judged, as well as reminding them that God is Creator, judge, and sustainer.

Peter's words are timely ones for the church today. More than any other time in history, believers in the West have easy access to the truth. Many of us have multiple copies of the Word of God in our homes, as well as other great resources to teach us the truths of the faith. Yet many believers seem to be illiterate when it comes to the Word of God. Scoffers who follow their own sinful desires have crept into Christian media, literature, and teaching because some believers are not steeped in the Scriptures as they should be. The antidote to ignorance and immorality is immersion in Scripture. As we know God as Creator, judge, and sustainer through His Word, we recognize those who deliberately overlook Him as such. We must respond to deliberate overlooking of truth with deliberate looking at truth. That means we should diligently be in the Word of God every day, asking the Lord to teach us sound doctrine, reprove us, correct us, and train us in righteousness (see 2 Tim. 3:16).

## II. Remember the Promise of His Coming Again: The Patience of God (3:8–13)

Peter reminds us in these verses that the Lord is not just the Creator, the judge of the living and the dead, and the sustainer of the universe, but He is also the promise keeper who is patient. Peter picks up on his previous phrase regarding the false teachers, "for this they willfully forget" (3:5), and turns it into an exhortation for believers: "But, beloved, do not forget this one thing" (3:8). The "one thing" he is referring to is that the Lord's time is not our time. He references Psalm 90, which is a prayer of Moses.

In the original context, Moses begins by exalting the Lord as the everlasting God. In contrast, man is like dust, and his life span is short. Moses knows that apart from God's mercy man would be consumed by His wrath. He also knows that man needs wisdom and God's favor to live well, so he prays that the Lord would teach us to number our days and establish the work of our hands.

Peter specifically references Psalm 90:4:

> For a thousand years in Your sight
> Are like yesterday when it is past,
> And like a watch in the night.

Peter is reminding his readers that contrary to the assumption and accusation of the false teachers, the Lord is on a different timetable from mankind because He is Lord of time. Contrary to being a slow promise keeper, He is a steadfast promise keeper who is patient as He carries out His plan of salvation. Like a kind and tender father, He doesn't want any of His creatures to perish. Instead, He wants to see them come to repentance.

A beautiful testimony of God's patience is found in the Old Testament book of Jonah. Jonah was called to reflect the heart of God and take the message of salvation to the Ninevites, but instead he reflected the heart of man and desired swift judgment for them. The Lord taught him a profound and powerful lesson through stormy seas, the belly of a whale, and a plant. He taught him the truth of Exodus 34:6–7: "The LORD, the LORD God, merciful and gracious, longsuffering, and abounding in goodness and truth, keeping mercy for thousands, forgiving iniquity and transgression and sin, by no means clearing the guilty, visiting the iniquity of the fathers upon the children and the children's children to the third and fourth generation." Like the passage in Peter, this verse in Exodus juxtaposes God's longsuffering and love with His judgment.

Although the Lord wishes that none would perish but that all would come to repentance, it will not be so. The flood of Noah's day has already displayed the truth that not all mankind will repent. However, believers should hope and pray that the unbelievers they know will come to saving faith. We should be patient and kind toward them, acknowledging the Lord is the one who saves and pointing them to Him. This can be extremely difficult to do at times, especially in the face of evil. Habakkuk's prophetic word provides encouragement for such times:

> Though it tarries, wait for it;
> Because it will surely come,
> It will not tarry.
>
> Behold the proud,
> His soul is not upright in him;
> But the just shall live by his faith. (2:3–4)

We live by faith in the Son of God who has promised to come again.

As an apostle of Christ, Peter had the privilege of learning at his Master's feet about many things, but important for us in this passage is his learning about Jesus's second coming. The Lord had taught him that the day of the Lord would come like a thief in the night (Matt. 24:43–44). Peter used imagery common to both the Old (see Isa. 34:4; 51:6) and New Testaments (see Rev. 20:11; 21:1) and reminded his readers that the earth as they knew it would be changed. Like the water of Noah's day that brought both judgment and renewal, so too the fire Peter speaks of will bring both judgment and renewal. The Lord will renew His creation, restoring its glory.

In poignant imagery that recalls the power and intensity of God's holiness (see Ex. 19; Heb. 12:18–29), Peter reminds believers that the earth and the works done on it will be exposed. No one can hide from the holy God. His eyes see all, and exposure is certain to come. Peter wants his readers to be ready, having nothing to hide, and lead holy lives before the One who has saved them and enabled them to be holy.

Holiness and godliness are chief concerns for Peter as his readers live in light of Christ's return. The false teachers assume their deeds don't matter because there will be no one before whom to give an account. Peter knows better. He knows that our deeds will be exposed, but he also knows that judgment day is not the end for believers. Christ's return is purposeful. He is coming again not only to judge unbelievers but also to save those who are eagerly waiting for Him in order to usher them into the new heavens and new earth in which righteousness dwells (see Isa. 65:17; 66:22; Rev. 21:1–22:5). Christ Himself is our bridegroom, and the church His bride. He is the one who is readying us for the big wedding day (see Eph. 5:25–27). The promise is sure to come, and we are to be ready.

Holiness and godliness are the result of saving faith. The Lord doesn't save us from our sin to leave us in our sin. He saves us in order to transform us more and more into the image of God. Such transformation won't be complete until glory, but it begins now, and because of God's divine power, holiness and godliness should flow from the hearts and lives of believers in increasing measure.

One of the most difficult things for me to do is to keep an eternal perspective in the midst of the pressures of daily life. The pressure seems to pull my eyes away from Christ, so my prayer is constantly, "Father, rivet my eyes on my Redeemer!" Kindness and patience are not my first instinct in the face of being wronged, and yet I am called to reflect the kindness and patience of the Lord. I often seem far from holy and godly in the midst of hurdles and children crying, "Give me!" But Peter is quick to remind us that the rescue for those drowning in the mundane is to wait for and hasten the day of God, resting in the eternal promises that have secured for us a future inheritance in the new heavens and new earth where you and I will be made perfectly righteous and will dwell forever with the triune God.

## III. Remember the Promise of His Coming Again: The Salvation of God (3:14–16)

Precisely because we have God's promise of salvation, including new heavens and a new earth, Peter urges us to be presently diligent in our devotion to purity and peace. Drawing from imagery related to the Old Testament sacrificial system, Peter charges his readers to be without spot and blameless. Such a charge is grounded in his previous teaching that Christ is the lamb without spot or blemish (see 1 Peter 1:19). It is Christ who is making us without spot or blemish (see Eph. 5:25–27). Peter's charge for purity stands against the false teachers who are "spots and blemishes, carousing in their own deceptions while they feast" in the midst of the covenant community (see 2 Peter 2:13). In contrast, believers are to present their bodies to the Lord as an unblemished, pure, and clean living sacrifice. We can do that only by being in Christ, who has given the perfect and final sacrifice of Himself on our behalf. We are clean and pure in Him and are being transformed more and more into the image of His purity daily.

Peter also charges his readers to be at peace not only with God, which has already been granted to them as believers (see Rom. 5:1), but also with one another. Peace with others flows from the peace we have with God. Since Christ has reconciled us to God the Father, we know true peace. No longer are we strangers and aliens, but we have been brought near to God through the cross of Christ. We have the privilege to share the opportunity for such peace with those who do not know it by proclaiming the gospel to them. In a world that often offers peace through ten steps, we bring the good news that true Peace has stepped down to us from heaven.

Unlike Jonah, who was angered by the Lord's patience toward the Ninevites (see Jonah 4), believers are to count the Lord's patience as salvation, a truth in which we should rejoice. We too should desire to see our lost neighbors, friends, and loved ones come to Christ, even if that means we must endure suffering a little longer. We have only to look to our persecuted brothers and sisters to see a beautiful example of such endurance. Many of them remain in their country despite persecution, praying for those who persecute them to come to saving faith, while worshiping, working, and witnessing for the kingdom of God. We must pray for them as they have requested, partnering with them through prayer and the desire to see the salvation of those who are still enemies of the faith.

It is not just those who persecute us that we should desire to be saved though. We should also pray that the ignorant and unstable twisters of Scripture come to saving faith. Peter and Paul both wrote with wisdom from above, speaking of the longsuffering of the Lord as salvation. While Peter acknowledges that there are some things Paul writes that are difficult to understand, he does not let the false teachers off the hook. Instead, he exposes their ignorance and instability. Not only do they twist Paul's words, they also twist other Scriptures, promoting a lawlessness that ends in licentiousness.

I was reminded of the twisting of Scripture when I was in seminary. One of my assignments for a theology class was to visit some places of worship that were different from my own. One of my choices was a large congregation of professing homosexuals. After the service I visited the bookstore. In it were several pieces of literature advocating that the Bible was pro-gay. One of the examples they used was the friendship of Jonathan and David. I was stunned as I flipped through some of the writings to see how erroneous their views were. Their ignorance and instability in the faith had led to lawlessness and licentiousness. I was deeply grieved that so many souls were being destroyed instead of delivered by the truth of salvation. That is why Peter turns in his final verses to exhort us to stay stable in the faith.

## IV. Remember the Promise of His Coming Again: The Glory of God (3:17–18)

In these final verses, Peter emphatically asserts that his readers ("*You* therefore, beloved" [v. 17, emphasis added]), in contrast to the twisters of Scripture ("as *they* do also the rest of the Scriptures" [v. 16, emphasis added]), are to make every effort not only to be stable in the faith but also to grow in the grace and knowledge of Jesus Christ. Peter knows that the key to keep from drifting from truth is to grow in truth. If we are not growing in the faith, we can be certain that we are drifting from it. That is why it is so important for believers to immerse themselves in the means of grace—the Word of God, the sacraments, and prayer.

One of Peter's readers' primary motivations for growing should be the reality that false teachers have twisted Scriptures to their own destruction. In contrast, believers are to be knowledgeable and stable. Peter exhorts them to grow in the grace and knowledge of Christ. Peter doesn't elaborate on what it means to grow in the grace and knowledge of Jesus Christ because he has taken time in both his letters to proclaim the true grace of God and the knowledge of the gospel (see 1 Peter 5:12).

We grow in the grace of Christ by living out what has already been given to us in the power of the gospel. We grow in the knowledge of Jesus Christ by walking in His ways and growing in our affection for Him. Because He is deserving of all glory, we should not be remiss to worship Him, work for His kingdom, and witness of His goodness in word and work to a watching world. Far from promoting erroneous teaching, we should proclaim the truth of Scripture. Far from proclaiming lawlessness, we should proclaim the good news that Jesus has fulfilled the law perfectly on our behalf. In gratitude for His deliverance of us from misery, we should grow in both the objective and the subjective grace and knowledge of Christ, not just knowing about Him and His grace, but growing in our experience of it as well.

At the close of his letter, Peter focuses believers' attention on the glory of God. It should be the chief goal of every believer to glorify God and enjoy Him forever. Believers can't add to God's glory, but they can proclaim His glory and praise His glorious name. In contrast to the teaching of the false teachers, who steal glory from God, Peter gives glory to God, specifically God the Son, both in the present and in the future. He is boldly proclaiming that far from being a promise breaker, Christ is a promise keeper who is active both now and to the day of eternity.

Before closing our study on 2 Peter, I want to ask you two important questions. First, do you love Jesus more than anyone or anything else in this world? Second, do you recognize that God's grace conforms you to the holiness and godliness of Christ? Often people fall off balance with one or the other. Some people say they love Jesus but live as they please. Other people work so hard at holiness by their own efforts that they forget God is the one who has the power to change us. The Bible is clear that our love for Jesus and the life we live before Him go hand in hand. Saving faith does not leave us as sinners. It delivers us from sin to make us more and more like God's Son. Peter heralds the call to make sure our lips (what we confess) and our lives (how we behave) line up. We are to glorify God so that others may see our good works and give praise to His holy name.

I am sure you can relate to my impatience in the midst of waiting for God's will to unfold. Let us no longer be tempted to exchange the true riches of the eternal for the false riches of the temporal. Let us stop running ahead of the Lord's timing in order to secure our own desired outcomes. Let us no longer think that the Lord has forgotten His promise to work all things out in our lives for our good and His glory. Let us stop overlooking the fact that the Lord has His own timetable, and it is not our own. Let us no longer think that we love our loved ones and desire their salvation more than the Lord does. Let us stop thinking that our ways are better than His. And let us no longer secure our own glory instead of giving glory to Him. As we wait, let us worship God, accept His plan, invite Him to be Lord over our situation, and trust Him with the outcome. Let us be women who grow in the grace and knowledge of Jesus Christ, recognizing that His divine power has given us all that we need to live lives of holiness and godliness for His glory.

I close with a passage from Habakkuk 3:17–19, one of my favorites during seasons of waiting:

> Though the fig tree may not blossom,
> Nor fruit be on the vines;
> Though the labor of the olive may fail,
> And the fields yield no food;
> Though the flock be cut off from the fold,
> And there be no herd in the stalls—
> Yet I will rejoice in the LORD,
> I will joy in the God of my salvation.
>
> The LORD God is my strength;
> He will make my feet like deer's feet,
> And He will make me walk on my high hills.

# Processing It Together...

1. What do we learn about God in 2 Peter 3:1–18?

2. How does this reshape how we should view our present circumstances?

3. What do we learn about God's Son, Jesus Christ?

4. How should this impact our relationship with God and with others?

5. What do we learn about God's covenant with His people?

6. How are we to live in light of this?

7. How can we apply 2 Peter 3:1–18 to our lives today and in the future?

8. How should we apply these verses in our churches?

9. Looking back at "Put It in Perspective" in your personal study questions, what did you find challenging or encouraging about this lesson?

10. Looking back at "Principles and Points of Application," how has this lesson impacted your life?

# Jude

## Preserved for Jesus Christ

# Introduction to Jude

Sweeping across America today is a call to surrender our fight for absolute truth, accepting instead the plurality of beliefs in our society as valid ways of salvation and giving up the persuasive arguments that Jesus is the only way to heaven. Churches have not been immune to such pervasive teaching, and indeed some have succumbed to pressure, turning their backs on truth to embrace error. It would be appropriate, then, for the book of Jude to be one of the most frequently taught books in the Bible today, yet it often gets overlooked. A Bible reader can easily miss this book of a mere twenty-five verses if she doesn't turn the page carefully from the letters of John before coming to the book of Revelation. Furthermore, Jude, though brief, is packed with difficult allusions that leave some Bible students confused, and this contributes to its not being used often in Bible studies and sermons today. But Jude is a book desperately needed in our age, for it heralds the battle cry to contend for and continue in the faith. The church today needs both messages.

First, in our postmodern culture, we need a fresh call to contend for the faith. Too often we forget that we must fight for the faith that we hold so dear in the midst of perverse teachings of grace that have crept into our churches unnoticed. Too often we readily accept the idea that we have no business telling someone else their faith won't get them to heaven, and so we fail to challenge pluralism with absolute truth.

Second, we need a fresh call to continue in the faith in our postmodern culture. Even though we have tremendous resources available to help us grow in our faith, many American Christians are becoming increasingly stagnant in it. Tragically, as we become dull toward truth, we readily accept error and end up perverting the true grace of God and denying Christ as Master and Lord.

Jude sounds the battle cry to do both, basing his call to action in God's covenantal love. First, he tells us who we are in light of who God is. Then, he calls us to contend for the faith and to continue in it. The order is important in our performance-driven culture today. Jude lifts our eyes from our own boots to the Beloved, centering our thoughts on His glory and majesty and dominion and authority, so that we are equipped soldiers to fight for the faith and remain firm in it.

## The Author, Date, and Audience of Jude

The divine author of Scripture is God Himself: "All Scripture is given by inspiration of God, and is profitable for doctrine, for reproof, for correction, for instruction in righteousness, that the man of God may be complete, thoroughly equipped for every good work" (2 Tim. 3:16–17). But the Holy Spirit used human authors to speak and write the Word of God (2 Peter 1:21).

The human author of the book of Jude is the younger brother of Jesus and James, the author of the book of James and one of the pillars in the early church (see Mark 6:1–6; Acts 15:13–21; Gal. 2:9–10; James 1:1). Jude was not a follower of Jesus during His earthly life and ministry (see John 7:5). It was only after the resurrection that he came to saving faith (see Acts 1:12–14). Yet God, in His grace, used one of Jesus's own biological brothers, whose eyes were blinded while his Savior walked this earth, as an instrument of the truth to help open up others' blind eyes.

Due to the similarity in content, Jude was most likely written around the same time as 2 Peter. Some commentators argue that Peter used Jude in writing 2 Peter; other commentators argue that Jude used 2 Peter in writing the book of Jude. Since Peter's martyrdom occurred in the mid-60s and 2 Peter was written just before his martyrdom, a date in the mid-60s for the composition of Jude is most likely.

It is hard to determine the audience to whom Jude was writing, although the letter reveals that he was writing to a specific church, or group of churches, in which certain ungodly people had crept unnoticed who were perverting the grace of God into sensuality and denying Christ as Master and Lord (see v. 4). Due to the many references to the Old Testament and to Jewish literature in this letter, it seems likely that Jude's readers were Jewish Christians. Perhaps the lack of morality of the ungodly points in the direction that these Jewish Christians were living in a largely Gentile area, but we cannot determine the exact location.

## The Purpose of Jude

The overarching purpose of Jude is stated clearly in his letter: "I found it necessary to write to you exhorting you *to contend earnestly for the faith* which was once for all delivered to the saints" (v. 3, emphasis added). Jude's purpose in writing must be seen in the broader context of his audience. He both opens and closes his letter by reminding his readers that they are "preserved in Jesus Christ" and that God "is able to keep [them] from stumbling" (vv. 1, 24). Sandwiched in between these two encouragements is the exhortation to "keep yourselves in the love of God" (v. 21). We might state the purpose this way, then: those who are preserved for Jesus Christ and kept by God from stumbling are to keep themselves in the love of God and contend for the faith.

The purpose of Jude becomes even clearer when we look at some key verses in his letter.

- He reminds his readers who they are—called, beloved in God the Father, and preserved for Jesus Christ—and whose they are—they belong to the One who is able to keep them from stumbling and to present them faultless before His glory with great joy (vv. 1, 24).

- He extends mercy, peace, and love to his readers, just as the Lord had extended mercy, peace, and love to him and just as he exhorts his readers to show mercy, peace, and love to others (vv. 2, 20–23).

- He exhorts us to contend for the faith in light of the ungodly scoffers who have crept into the churches (vv. 3–4, 17–19).

- He reminds his readers of the judgment of God that falls upon the ungodly by using examples from the past in order to warn of judgment on the ungodly in the future (vv. 5–16).

**An Outline of Jude**

Different and more detailed outlines of Jude can be found in commentaries, but for this Bible study, I suggest the following:

I.   A Call to Contend for the Faith (vv. 1–16)

II.  A Call to Continue in the Faith (vv. 17–25)

Each lesson will further divide this broad outline into smaller parts, but for now, note these major divisions in your mind as you prepare to study Jude.

Now that we have reviewed the author, date, and audience of Jude and considered its purpose and outline, let's also review "An Overview of the History of Redemption and Revelation" on pages xvi–xxi and "A Christ-Centered Interpretation of 1 Peter, 2 Peter, and Jude" on pages xxi–xxiii in the introduction to this Bible study. It is important to keep these matters in mind as we take a closer look at Jude.

Perhaps you have given up the fight for the faith today, subtly accepting our culture's call to embrace pluralism. Or maybe you have slipped from your belief in the central doctrines of the faith and are following a different way instead. Perhaps you have given up Bible study for some time now due to difficult seasons in life and need to commit again to a steadfast study of Scripture. Or maybe you need a fresh reminder that false teaching is still alive and well in churches today. Perhaps you need to remember how great God is in the midst of a society that relegates Him to another option in the pool of pluralism. Regardless, Jude has a timely word for all of us. He calls us to contend for the faith and to remain in it while at the same time grounding us in the greatness and eternality of God's glory and majesty and dominion and power.

# A Call to Contend for the Faith

Jude 1–16

$\mathcal{P}$*urpose*...

**Head.** What do I need to know from this passage in Scripture?

- Judgment is certain for those who pervert the grace of God and deny Jesus Christ.

**Heart.** How does what I learn from this passage affect my internal relationship with the Lord?

- I am a kingdom disciple who rightly proclaims the grace of God and acknowledges Jesus Christ as my Master and Lord.

**Hands.** How does what I learn from this passage translate into action for God's kingdom?

- I will extend mercy, peace, and love to others.
- I will contend for the faith in the presence of the ungodly.
- I will fully learn, remember, and teach others the central doctrines of the Christian faith.
- I will seek holiness, not licentiousness.
- I will lovingly lead those under my authority in the grace and knowledge of Jesus Christ.

# Personal Study...

**Pray.** Ask that God will open up your heart and mind as you study His Word. This is His story of redemption that He has revealed to us, and the Holy Spirit is our teacher.

**Ponder the Passage.** Read Jude in its entirety. Then reread Jude verses 1–16.

- *Point.* What is the point of this passage? How does this relate to the point of the entire book?

- *People.* Who are the main people involved in this passage? What characterizes them?

- *Persons of the Trinity.* Where do you see God the Father, God the Son, and God the Holy Spirit in this passage?

- *Puzzling Parts.* Are there any parts of the passage that you don't quite understand or that seem interesting or confusing?

**Put It in Perspective.**

- *Place in Scripture.* What is the original context of this text? What is the redemptive-historical context—what has or hasn't happened in redemptive history at this point in Scripture? How does this text connect to Christ?

*The following questions will help if you got stuck on any of the previous questions, and they will help you dig a little deeper into the text, putting it all into perspective.*

**1. vv. 1–2.** (a) How does Jude identify himself?

(b) What do you learn about Jude from Matthew 13:53–58; Mark 6:1–6; John 7; Acts 1:12–14; and 1 Corinthians 9:5?

(c) Why would it have been advantageous for Jude to mention that he was a brother of James (see Acts 15:13–21; Gal. 2:9–10; James 1:1)?

(d) How does Jude describe the recipients of his letter?

(e) What language does Jude use that suggests he is alluding to Isaiah 41:9; 42:1, 6; 43:4; 48:12, 15; 49:1, 8; and 54:5–6?

(f) What language does he use at the end of his letter that is similar (vv. 24–25)?

(g) What does Jude proclaim to his readers?

**2. vv. 3–4.** (a) How does Jude address his readers, and what does this reveal about him?

(b) What was Jude very eager to write about?

(c) What did he find it necessary to write about instead?

(d) Why did his plans change?

(e) How does Jude describe the people about whom he is warning his readers?

**3. vv. 5–7.** (a) What did Jude's readers once fully know, and of what do they now need to be reminded?

(b) Why is it significant that Jude tells us Jesus ("the Lord" in the NKJV) saved Israel out of Egypt (see Ex. 12:33–15:21)?

(c) Why did Jesus ("the Lord" in the NKJV) bring destruction on some of the people (see also Num. 14:11–12)?

(d) The exodus generation is the first example of God's judgment in these verses. What is the second example?

(e) Why were the angels judged, and what is their doom?

(f) What is the third example of God's judgment in these verses (see also Gen. 18:16–19:29)?

(g) Why were these cities judged, and what is their doom?

4. **vv. 8–10.** (a) How does Jude compare the false teachers of his day with the three examples in verses 5–7?

(b) What do you learn about the archangel Michael from Daniel 10:13, 21; 12:1; and Revelation 12:7–9?

(c) To whom does the archangel Michael leave judgment (see also Zech. 3:1–2)?

(d) How does Jude use the archangel Michael to point out the false teachers' error? How does Michael contrast with the false teachers?

**5. vv. 11–13.** (a) How does Jude's "woe" recall the judgment pronounced by the Old Testament prophets (see, for example, Isa. 5:8–30)?

(b) To what three examples from the Old Testament does Jude compare the false teachers?

(c) What do you learn about the way of Cain from Genesis 4:1–26; Hebrews 11:4; and 1 John 3:12?

(d) What do you learn about Balaam's error from Numbers 22–24; 31:16; Deuteronomy 23:3–6; Joshua 13:22; 24:9–10; Nehemiah 13:1–2; Micah 6:5; 2 Peter 2:15; and Revelation 2:14?

(e) What do you learn about Korah's rebellion in Numbers 16:1–50 and 26:10–11?

(f) List the metaphors Jude uses to describe the false teachers.

(g) Read Ezekiel 34:2, 8–10, 18–19. To whom is Jude alluding when he accuses the false teachers of "serving only themselves"?

(h) What is the doom of these false teachers?

**6. vv. 14–16.** (a) What do you learn about Enoch from Genesis 5:18–24?

(b) What did Enoch prophesy about the false teachers of Jude's day?

(c) What are some examples Jude gives of the false teachers' ungodliness?

(d) Who are the false teachers really grumbling against (see Num. 14:26–35)?

**7.** In contrast to the false teachers, find a passage of Scripture that shows how Jesus is

(a) submissive to authority

(b) pure

(c) the good teacher

(d) the Good Shepherd

(e) humble

(f) one who does not show favoritism

**Principles and Points of Application.**

**8. vv. 1–2.** (a) Would you describe yourself and would others describe you as a bond-servant of Jesus Christ? Why or why not?

(b) How has the Lord multiplied mercy, peace, and love to you this week?

**9. vv. 3–4.** (a) In what ways do you need to contend for the faith in your present circumstances?

(b) How do some people today, who claim to be Christians, pervert the grace of God and deny Christ?

(c) How are you on guard against false teaching?

**10. vv. 5–7.** (a) In what ways are you tempted to abdicate authority (by not keeping your "proper domain") and indulge in sexual immorality?

(b) Spend time today in prayer, asking the Lord to help you turn from these temptations.

(c) Spend time today in prayer for those you know who are in rebellion against the Lord.

**11. vv. 8–10.** (a) In what ways are you tempted to judge other people instead of leaving judgment to the Lord?

(b) Ask the Lord to help you leave judgment to Him so that you are free to extend mercy, peace, and love to others.

**12. vv. 11–13.** (a) In what ways are you tempted to compare yourself to others?

(b) In what ways are you tempted toward monetary gain?

(c) In what ways are you grumbling and complaining in your present circumstances?

(d) Ask the Lord to purify your heart so that you might bear fruit for His glory.

**13. vv. 14–16.** (a) In what areas of your life would you or others say you are grumbling? Discontent? Following your own sinful desires? Proud? Showing favoritism to gain advantage?

(b) Repent of these today, and then pray for the Lord to fill you with contentment, pure desires, humility, and impartiality.

# Putting It All Together...

We are having a crisis of biblical literacy in our day. Ironic, isn't it? We have more resources readily available to us than previous generations, yet many churchgoers do not fully know the central doctrines of the Christian faith or how to define the true grace of God. Perhaps we have so many resources available that the Bible has just become another book like all the others, read once and then shelved until we desire to pick it up and peruse it again for whatever reason. Or perhaps we have been so overloaded with information that we don't fully remember anything because we are always pushing things out of our minds to make room for more.

Whatever the reason our knowledge has become dull, the result has been disastrous. We have churches proclaiming a false gospel, perverting the grace of God into licentiousness and denying Christ as Master and Lord. People today are fine with a savior, but they flee from a master. They want nothing to do with absolute authority in their lives. They want to be their own masters.

The problem is not new, and neither is the solution. The problem of perverting the grace of God has existed since the fall of mankind. But the solution has also been proclaimed since the fall of mankind. In seed form, the gospel is proclaimed in the context of the Lord God bringing judgment upon the serpent for deceiving Eve in Genesis 3:15:

> And I will put enmity
> Between you and the woman,
> And between your seed and her Seed;
> He shall bruise your head,
> And you shall bruise His heel.

As the history of redemption moves forward, we see the gospel in seed form grow until the climax of redemptive history comes in Christ's life, death, resurrection, and ascension, and the apostles proclaim the gospel in its fullness. The solution to denying Christ as Master and Lord is exalting Him as such. The solution to perverting the grace of God is proclaiming the true grace of God. Jude helps us with both.

## I. A Call to Contend for the Faith: A Reason (vv. 1–4)

Jude begins by telling us that he is a "bondservant of Jesus Christ" (v. 1). Being a servant of Jesus Christ, the highest and greatest Master (see v. 4), carried much weight. As one who served Christ, Jude had devoted his life to accepting His plans and following His words (see Luke 1:38). As a servant of Christ, Jude was also one to whom others should listen since he spoke on behalf of the King.

To learn more about Jude, we must turn to other parts of the New Testament. The Gospels tell us that Jude was one of Jesus's brothers who did not believe He was the Promised One, the Messiah, during the time of His earthly ministry (see Matt. 13:53–58; Mark 6:1–6; John 7). Sometime after Jesus's death, however, and before the day of Pentecost, Jesus's brothers came to believe that He was the Christ, the Son of the living God, for they were together with the early church, praying in the upper room when the disciples returned to Jerusalem after seeing Jesus ascend into heaven (see Acts 1:12–14).

Jude was also the brother of James, likely younger than James (see Matt. 13:55). It would have been advantageous for Jude to mention his association with James to his readers since James was one of the prominent leaders of the New Testament church and had also written a letter to the churches (see Acts 15:13–21; Gal. 2:9–10; James 1:1). It is amazing grace when we remember as we read the books of James and Jude that these two brothers of Jesus were not even saved during His earthly ministry, yet God called them out of their darkness after Jesus's death and then, by the Holy Spirit, inspired them to write two of the letters that have been preserved as part of the Scriptures.

Jude writes to believers and describes his readers in three ways that recall God's relationship with the Old Testament church. First, they are called. God has called them out of His free love to be a people set apart for Himself (see Ex. 6:2–9; Deut. 7:6–8; Isa. 41:9; 42:1, 6; 48:12, 15; 49:1). Second, they are God's beloved. God the Father has purposed the salvation of His people, a people whom He loves as a husband loves his wife (see Isa. 43:4; 54:5; Zeph. 3:17). Finally, they are preserved by God's promises for Jesus Christ (see Isa. 49:8–10, 15–16). In the New Testament, we learn that the church (the bride of Christ) is being readied to meet her husband (Christ). Paul tells us that Christ is sanctifying the church, preparing her to be His bride (Eph. 5:25–27). The apostle John also picks up this imagery in speaking of the day when Christ will return: "Then, I, John, saw the holy city, New Jerusalem, coming down out of heaven from God, prepared as a bride adorned for her husband" (Rev. 21:2).

Jude extends a prayer to his readers. Knowing they have already received mercy, peace, and love as those who are called, beloved, and preserved, he prays that these things will be multiplied to them. He wants them to know more and more of the mercy of God, the peace of God, and the love of God. We will learn in his letter that these are exactly the things the ungodly are trying to steal, kill, and destroy in the midst of them (see vv. 12, 19, 21–23). Jude is concerned that such a threat be exposed—so concerned that he changes the intention of his letter.

Jude closes his introduction to his letter by giving us the reason for his writing. Although Jude wanted to write to his readers about their common salvation, he found it necessary (in light of the false teachers who had crept into the churches) to exhort them to contend for the faith instead. The word for "contend" was often used in Greek literature in relation to the contests in the stadium.[1] In other words, Jude was exhorting them to nothing less than fighting for the faith. He writes as a pastor who cares for his sheep, but he is well aware that he is writing on behalf of the Chief Shepherd, who loves His sheep much more than he ever could (notice he addresses them as "beloved" in vv. 3 and 17). Jude is not writing about an empty set of rules and rituals, but the faith that had been delivered to the saints once for all—the apostles' teaching that carried the authority of the word of God. This faith centered on the life, death, resurrection,

---

1. Peter H. Davids, *The Letters of 2 Peter and Jude*, The Pillar New Testament Commentary (Grand Rapids: Eerdmans, 2006), 42.

and ascension of Jesus Christ as well as the promise that He is coming again to judge the living and the dead. Such teaching preserves the true grace of God, which leads to sanctification, instead of perverting it, which leads to sensuality. Such teaching also dignifies our only Master and Lord, Jesus Christ, instead of denying Him.

Perversion of the grace of God and a denial of Jesus Christ as Lord and Master were not limited to Jude's day. Such problems remain in our churches today. One of the greatest dangers of these problems is their subtlety. Ungodliness creeps in so quietly that it goes unnoticed. That is why it is so important to be grounded in the faith so that we recognize falsehood. If we don't know the faith, then we can't contend for the faith. The greatest way for us to know the faith is to be immersed in the study of Scripture. Such a means of grace is one of the ways the Lord multiplies mercy, peace, and love to us. In the study of God's Word, we also learn that we are called by God, beloved in God the Father, and kept for God the Son. We have become servants of the greatest Master and Lord of all, Jesus Christ, and we are to contend for the glory of His name. Jude's reason for writing should be our reason for writing, speaking, and teaching others today. We are to contend for the faith so that God may be glorified and Christ exalted.

## II. A Call to Contend for the Faith: A Reminder (vv. 5–10)

Jude transitions from giving his readers a reason for his writing to a reminder. Interestingly, it is a reminder of what they once fully knew. Jude wants his readers to be reminded of one of the central doctrines of the faith—the judgment of God. Their knowledge of God's judgment had become so dull that they didn't notice the ungodly people in their midst who were perverting God's grace and denying Christ.

Jude uses three examples from the Old Testament to remind his readers of God's judgment. First, Jude recalls the exodus generation. The Lord Jesus had delivered Israel out of Egypt in order to be God's treasured possession. Because they were His people, He gave them laws. These laws not only told the people how they were to live as servants of their King but they also revealed the holiness of their Creator and Redeemer. One of God's promises to His people was to give them the land of Canaan. But in between Egypt and Canaan lay the wilderness. The wilderness became a time of testing for Israel. Would they look in faith toward Canaan, or would they turn back in disbelief toward Egypt? There were many who grumbled and complained against Moses in the wilderness, but they were ultimately grumbling and complaining against the Lord. Such discontentment was rooted in unbelief. And the consequence of unbelief was nothing less than death (see Num. 14:35).

Second, Jude recalls the rebellious angels. This example stems from a Jewish interpretation of Genesis 6:1–4. In Genesis 6 we read of "the sons of God" and "the daughters of men" bearing children together.[2] The context of these verses is the wickedness of

---

2. Much of the ancient Jewish literature interpreted these "sons of God" to be angels. The book of 1 Enoch, which Jude quotes in verses 14–15, describes the story of the fallen angels who came to earth and took human wives. Together they bore evil children (the giants). The judgment for such sin was the

man and the judgment of God. In this case the judgment came in the form of a flood. Only eight persons (Noah and his family) were saved. Jude's point in using the angels as an illustration is their rebellion against authority. They left the position of authority that they had been granted. Such rebellion was costly. They are being kept for judgment on the final day.

Third, Jude recalls the wicked cities of Sodom and Gomorrah, as well as the cities that surrounded them. Genesis describes the wickedness of these cities, which Jude specifically notes were known for sexual immorality (see Gen. 18–19). These cities also serve as an example of God's judgment upon those who rebel against His order—punishment of eternal fire.

Jude compares the ungodly people in his readers' midst with these three Old Testament examples. Like the unbelieving exodus generation, the rebellious angels, and the sexually immoral cities, the ungodly in their midst relied on their dreams instead of true revelation, defiled the flesh instead of living in purity before the holy God, rejected authority instead of submitting to God's authority, and blasphemed the angels ("dignitaries") instead of recognizing that God had given angels a position of authority in their proper dwelling.

In order to draw a contrast between the ungodly and the godly, Jude uses the example of the archangel Michael. We learn about Michael in the books of Daniel and Revelation. He is one of the chief princes who contended by Daniel's side when the prince of the kingdom of Persia withstood him (Dan. 10:13, 21). He is the great prince who has charge of God's people (Dan. 12:1). He is also said to be involved in the war that arose in heaven when Satan was defeated (Rev. 12:7–9).

We learn of Moses's death in Deuteronomy 34:5–8. In those verses we learn that "no one knows his grave to this day" (Deut. 34:6). It is not surprising, then, that interpretations arose among the Jews regarding what happened to his body. Jude alludes to one of these when he speaks of Michael disputing with the devil. The devil wanted the body of Moses, but Michael wouldn't let him have it. Yet, contrary to the rebellious angels and Satan (as well as the exodus generation and the wicked cities), Michael did not rebel against his position of authority as an angel but stayed within it, leaving judgment to the Lord: "The Lord rebuke you!" (v. 9). The latter is a direct quote from Zechariah 3:2. The context of this verse is the Lord rebuking Satan after he accused Joshua the high priest and promising to bring His servant, the Branch, to remove the iniquity of the land He had given His people (see Zech. 3:1–10). Unlike Michael, the ungodly people among Jude's readers are like the devil; they blaspheme God's supernatural order of things and are destroyed by their own fleshly desires.

Because we have been given the grace of God and because we are servants of our Master and Lord, Jesus Christ, we are to contend for the faith that has been handed down to us, including the doctrine of God's judgment. Churches today are increasingly

---

flood. Gene L. Green. *Jude & 2 Peter*, Baker Exegetical Commentary on the New Testament (Grand Rapids: Baker Academic, 2008), 67.

shying away from speaking about God's judgment lest it offend someone in the pew. But God has called us to teach the entirety of His Word, not just bits and pieces of it. We do not extend grace to others when we refuse to tell them the entirety of the gospel. Yes, Jesus saves, but Jesus also judges. We need to exhort one another to godly living and to revering the name of Christ as we eagerly await His return. For those who are in Christ Jesus, there will be no condemnation on the final day of judgment, for Christ has already paid for our sin. Like Joshua the high priest, we have been robed in new garments. These are not just new garments but Christ's garments, which will never stain because we wear Christ's righteousness.

### III. A Call to Contend for the Faith: A Reservation (vv. 11–13)

In the previous verses, Jude has clarified his reason for writing—to contend for the faith. He has reminded his readers of one of the central doctrines of the Christian faith—God's judgment. Now he moves on to speak of a reservation. Normally when we think of reservations we think of restaurants, hotels, and other special places that are important enough for us to visit that we have planned ahead and committed to going. Such places usually add good memories to our family scrapbook. But this is far from the kind of reservation Jude is speaking of in these verses. The reservation Jude pronounces is a reservation of judgment.

He begins with a woe reminiscent of the Old Testament prophets, who pronounced judgment on God's enemies as well as on His rebellious people (see, for example, Isa. 5:8–30). The woe is not spoken directly to the ungodly but rather to Jude's readers, serving as a warning. He again takes three examples from the Old Testament to prove the ungodliness of those who have crept into the church, perverting the grace of God and denying Christ.

First, he uses the example of Cain. We first learn of Cain in Genesis 4. He was Adam and Eve's firstborn son. Cain gave in to the sin of anger, which led him to murder his younger brother, Abel. Cain refused to be his brother's keeper and was cursed because of it (Gen. 4:1–26). The apostle John picks up the story line of Cain, using him as an example of what not to be like as a Christian. John tells us that Cain was of the Evil One and murdered his brother because his deeds were evil when his brother's were righteous (see 1 John 3:12). In contrast to Cain, Christians are to love one another. By using the example of Cain, Jude is exposing the error of the ungodly in the church's midst. Far from loving the brethren, they were promoting lies concerning the faith. Their deeds were evil, while the deeds of the godly were righteous.

Second, Jude uses the example of Balaam. The king of Moab asked Balaam to curse Israel for him since he was afraid he couldn't defeat them. God warned Balaam that he shouldn't curse Israel, because they were His blessed people. But the king was persistent, and Balaam went with the king's princes. Along the way the Lord used Balaam's donkey to reveal Balaam's anger and perverse way. When Balaam finally arrived, the king was expecting him to curse Israel, but instead the Lord used Balaam to pronounce a blessing on Israel (see Num. 22–24). Balaam also advised Israel to participate in pagan worship of Baal of Peor (Num. 25:1–3; 31:16), which resulted in a plague of judgment. Balaam became the epitome of false teachers since he taught the king of Moab to lead God's people into pagan idolatry and sexual immorality (Rev. 2:14). By using the example of Balaam, Jude continues to expose the errors of the ungodly in the church. They had forsaken the right way and gone astray, loving gain from wrongdoing (see 2 Peter 2:15).

Third, Jude uses the example of Korah's rebellion. We learn of Korah's rebellion in Numbers. Korah refused to submit to Moses and Aaron, those the Lord had placed over His people as leaders in the wilderness. Korah and the people who stood behind him wanted more honor for themselves than they had already received. Ultimately, they were rejecting the Lord's authority. Such rebellion brought severe judgment from the Lord (see Num. 16). By using the example of Korah's rebellion, Jude continues to expose the error of the ungodly. In their case, they too had rebelled against authority, even denying the Master and Lord, Jesus Christ.

In case we don't connect the dots between the Old Testament examples and the ungodly in the church during Jude's day, Jude lists several metaphors to describe them. First, they are spots at the church's love feasts. This goes back to the way of Cain. Instead of loving Abel, he hated him. The word *spots* can also be translated as "hidden reefs," which are dangerous to ships. They cause shipwrecks. For Jude's readers, the ungodly threatened to shipwreck their faith.

Second, they feast with the church without fear. This goes back to Korah's rebellion. They remained in the midst of Israel without fearing the authority God had placed over them. Such rebellion against authority is dangerous. It is rebellion against the Lord Himself.

Third, they serve only themselves. This can also be translated "shepherds feeding themselves." Such imagery references Ezekiel when he spoke about the bad shepherds of Israel who fed themselves instead of caring for God's people. The Lord brought judgment against them, putting a stop to their unrighteous ways and rescuing His sheep out of their mouths (see Ezek. 34:1–24). The ungodly in Jude's day, far from caring for the sheep in the congregation, were only seeking their own gain.

Fourth, they are waterless clouds. When rain is needed, a cloud holds hope for those waiting. Clouds that are waterless cannot provide the resource needed for growth. Proverbs 25:14 teaches us that "whoever falsely boasts of giving is like clouds and wind without rain." The ungodly were empty as well, providing nothing for the people to grow in their faith.

Fifth, they are carried about by winds. Like unstable and double-minded people, they are caught up in every wind of false doctrine. What is worse, they are beckoning others to be swept along with them.

Sixth, they are fruitless trees in late autumn, twice dead, and uprooted. At the very time they should be bearing mature and rich fruit, they prove to bear no fruit. Instead of helping others grow in the faith, they are hindering them, promoting a false gospel.

Seventh, they are raging waves of the sea. The Lord spoke through the prophet Isaiah declaring that there was no peace for the wicked. They are like the tossing sea that cannot be quiet; its waters toss up mire and dirt (see Isa. 57:20). Instead of keeping order in the church, the ungodly are bringing shame to the church by their immoral behavior and idolatrous words. This is nothing less than a perversion of the grace of God.

Finally, they are wandering stars. Instead of being a stable beacon of light, they flit and float from false doctrine to false doctrine, incurring judgment as they go. They pretend to guide others to great places, but in reality they lead them to falsehood and futility. In their pride they rise against God, seeking to be like Him, but their end will be nothing less than eternal punishment (see Isa. 14:12–15).

These verses should lead us to examine our churches and ourselves. Is our covenant community characterized by love or licentiousness? Do we promote ourselves and our ministries for the purpose of gaining a reputation and resources, or do we give glory to God in all things? Are we quick to submit to authority, or do we want to usurp it? Are we living out what we say we believe, or does our walk not line up with our talk? Remember, ungodliness creeps into our lives unnoticed. If we are not tethered to the truth, we will drift into deception.

## IV. A Call to Contend for the Faith: A Revelation (vv. 14–16)

Jude continues on from a reservation for judgment to a revelation of judgment. To prove his point that the ungodly will be judged, he cites a prophecy of Enoch. We first learn of Enoch in the book of Genesis. He was the seventh generation descended from Adam and was a man who walked with God. He lived for 365 years, and Moses tells us that then "God took him" rather than saying that he died (Gen. 5:21–24).

It is not surprising, then, that there is a book named after this man who walked with God and whom God took. The book of 1 Enoch is part of the Old Testament Pseudepigrapha, a noncanonical collection of works that date, for the most part, from before the time the New Testament books were written. Jude quotes from 1 Enoch in order to further his exhortation to his readers to contend for the faith. Thousands of years before the ungodly of Jude's day crept into the church, Enoch had already spoken of their certain judgment, looking ahead to a day of revelation of God's judgment. On that day their deeds of ungodliness will be revealed as well as their denunciation of the Master and Lord, Jesus Christ.

Jude spells out some of the words and works of the ungodly for us. First, they are murmurers. This was the sin of the wilderness generation. Although they murmured against Moses, they ultimately murmured against God, and they were judged for it (see, for example, Num. 14:26–35). Second, they are complainers. Instead of being content with their lot in life, which was given to them from the hand of God, they rebelled against it. Third, they walked according to their own lusts. Instead of seeking holiness in light of the true grace of God, they perverted the grace of God into sensuality. Fourth, they are loud-mouthed boasters. Instead of exalting the only Master and Lord, Jesus Christ, they exalted themselves. Finally, they flattered people to gain advantage. Instead of showing impartiality, they chose favorites in order to accelerate their own power, position, and prestige.

In stark contrast to the ungodly, Jesus "became for us wisdom from God—and righteousness and sanctification and redemption—that, as it is written, 'He who glories, let him glory in the LORD'" (1 Cor. 1:30–31). He left His place and position of authority for the right reasons, submitting to the purposes of His Father, coming in humility to accomplish the redemption of God's people. He walked in perfect purity and obedience to the law of God during His earthly life. He is the good teacher and the Good Shepherd. In fact, He is the Chief Shepherd. He does not show favoritism but instead created one new man from the two, so making peace, reconciling both Jews and Gentiles to God in one body through the cross of Calvary (Eph. 2:14–16).

As those who are in Christ, we are to show forth thanksgiving and contentment, seek purity in every area of our lives, humble ourselves before the Lord and before others, and show impartiality, recognizing that there are no favorites in the kingdom of God nor is there room for competition. Each of us has been given gifts to serve one another, not to gain advantage over one another.

There is no excuse for biblical illiteracy today. We need to challenge one another to be immersed in the Scriptures so that we are so familiar with the truth we immediately recognize error. We need to challenge one another to read and study the Bible more than any other book. We need to kindly confront one another when we turn the grace of God into licentiousness. And we need to exhort one another to exalt Jesus Christ as the Master and Lord of our lives.

# Processing It Together...

1. What do we learn about God in Jude verses 1–16?

2. How does this reshape how we should view our present circumstances?

3. What do we learn about God's Son, Jesus Christ?

4. How should this impact our relationship with God and with others?

5. What do we learn about God's covenant with His people?

6. How are we to live in light of this?

7. How can we apply Jude verses 1–16 to our lives today and in the future?

8. How should we apply these verses in our churches?

9. Looking back at "Put It in Perspective" in your personal study questions, what did you find challenging or encouraging about this lesson?

10. Looking back at "Principles and Points of Application," how has this lesson impacted your life?

# A Call to Continue in the Faith

Jude 17–25

*Purpose . . .*

**Head.** What do I need to know from this passage in Scripture?

- The Lord is able to keep me from stumbling and to present me blameless before His presence with great joy.

**Heart.** How does what I learn from this passage affect my internal relationship with the Lord?

- I am a kingdom disciple who remembers the truth, remains in the love of God, and rejoices in my Savior.

**Hands.** How does what I learn from this passage translate into action for God's kingdom?

- I will spend concentrated time studying Scripture so that I can recognize scoffers.

- I will help others strive toward holiness.

- I will engage in the means of grace with my church family.

- I will display mercy to those entangled in sin, pray for them, and proclaim the truth to them.

- I will rejoice with others in our common salvation purposed by the Father, accomplished by the Son, and applied by the Spirit.

# Personal Study...

**Pray.** Ask that God will open up your heart and mind as you study His Word. This is His story of redemption that He has revealed to us, and the Holy Spirit is our teacher.

**Ponder the Passage.** Read Jude verses 17–25.

- *Point.* What is the point of this passage? How does this relate to the point of the entire book?

- *People.* Who are the main people involved in this passage? What characterizes them?

- *Persons of the Trinity.* Where do you see God the Father, God the Son, and God the Holy Spirit in this passage?

- *Puzzling Parts.* Are there any parts of the passage that you don't quite understand or that seem interesting or confusing?

**Put It in Perspective.**

- *Place in Scripture.* Since you have studied Jude's place in Scripture in lesson 9, you may want to take this opportunity to review your answer.

*The following questions will help if you got stuck on any of the previous questions, and they will help you dig a little deeper into the text, putting it all into perspective.*

**1. vv. 17–19.** (a) How does Jude address his readers?

(b) What does he ask them to remember?

(c) How does Jude's quotation of what the apostles had spoken reflect Jesus's words in Matthew 24:11, 23–24; Mark 13:5–6, 21–22; and the apostles' words in Acts 20:29–30; 1 Timothy 4:1–3; 2 Timothy 3:1–5; 4:3–4; and 1 John 2:18, 22?

(d) What phrases does Jude use to characterize the mockers or, in some Bible translations, scoffers?

**2. vv. 20–21.** (a) How does Jude address his readers?

(b) What ways are Jude's readers to keep themselves in the love of God?

(c) How is the main clause of these verses, "keep yourselves in the love of God," related to what Jude has already written in verse 1, "preserved in Jesus Christ," and what he will close with in verse 24, "to Him who is able to keep you from stumbling"?

**3. vv. 22–23.** (a) In light of the mercy we will receive when Christ comes again, what does Jude call his readers to do?

(b) Read Zechariah 3:1–4. In what ways is Jude alluding to this passage in verse 23?

**4. vv. 24–25.** (a) What encouragement does Jude give his readers at the end of a letter that speaks of those who have stumbled and become defiled?

(b) How does "God our Savior" reflect Deuteronomy 32:15?

(c) How does the phrase "who alone is wise" reflect Deuteronomy 6:4–9; 11:13–21; and Numbers 15:37–41?

(d) Through what mediator are believers able to give praise to God (see also Heb. 13:15)?

(e) Why are the attributes of glory and majesty, as well as dominion and power, especially appropriate in light of Jude's letter?

(f) How does Jude emphasize God's past, present, and future glory and authority?

(g) What does the term *amen* mean?

**Principles and Points of Application.**

**5. vv. 17–19.** (a) How often do you spend time studying Scripture? What ways could you find to increase the time you spend studying Scripture?

(b) How has this study reminded you of the importance of being saturated in the Scriptures and committed to the way of the Lord?

(c) Have you witnessed divisive, worldly people who are devoid of the Spirit in churches today? How have they demonstrated their divisiveness and worldliness?

(d) It is easy to point our fingers at others, but in what ways have you contributed to divisiveness and worldliness in your spheres of influence?

**6. vv. 20–21.** (a) How does it encourage you that you are preserved in Jesus Christ, even as you are commanded to keep yourself in the love of God?

(b) Jude reminds us that faith is active when he exhorts us to keep ourselves in the love of God. He tells us we are to do this in three ways: (1) by building ourselves up in our most holy faith, (2) by praying in the Holy Spirit, and (3) by waiting for the mercy of our Lord Jesus Christ that leads to eternal life. How are you using the means of grace (Word, sacraments, and prayer) to grow in the faith? How often do you spend time in individual and corporate prayer? Are you waiting for Christ's return with hopeful expectation while sharing the gospel with others?

(c) How are you helping others to do the same?

**7. vv. 22–23.** (a) How do you respond to those who display doubt about central doctrines of the faith? How should you respond?

(b) In what ways are you willing to rub shoulders with sinners in order to show them their sin and point them to the Savior?

(c) How do you display mercy to those entangled in sin, specifically sexual sin, while at the same time being careful to not indulge in their sinful ways?

**8. vv. 24–25.** (a) In your present circumstances, how does it encourage you that God is able to keep you from stumbling and to present you blameless before His presence with great joy?

(b) Meditate on our Mediator Jesus Christ today and that He has made it possible for us to draw near to God in praise and thanksgiving.

(c) Write out a prayer of your own, exalting God's attributes, beginning with His glory, majesty, dominion, and power.

# Putting It All Together...

One of the deacons at my church is a firefighter. He also happens to be the husband of a dear friend of mine, so I have the opportunity to hang out with their family for fun things such as field trips with our children. On one occasion I asked him what the hardest thing about being a firefighter was for him. In the course of his answer, he admitted that he felt badly for getting a "high" from someone else's deepest tragedy. As he explained, I began to understand what he meant. He painted a picture for me in words of what it was like to receive a call to a fire in the middle of the night. As the fire truck cruised down the streets, he could see the blazing orange flames and billows of smoke ahead. Racing toward the fire, he was gearing up to do what he had been trained to do, which brought an adrenaline rush. No two fires were the same. There had been times in his past when he was not able to rescue someone out of the flames because it was too late—the person had already died. He said these occasions were some of the most difficult parts of his job. But other times, he was able to be an instrument God used to rescue someone.

The week of this conversation was the same week I was working on this lesson in Jude. I couldn't help but be reminded of Jude's exhortation to save others by "pulling them out of the fire" (v. 23). We are all called to be firefighters. As such, we must be trained, equipped, and clothed with Scripture. Like my friend's husband, there will be times when we are not able to rescue someone from the flames of addiction or despair, sensuality or distorted truth. But other times, by God's grace, the Lord will use us to snatch someone from the flames of sin, saving their souls.

**I. A Call to Continue in the Faith: Remember (vv. 17–19)**

In the closing section of his letter, Jude transitions from pronouncing judgment on the ungodly (who were perverting the grace of God into sensuality and denying Jesus Christ as Master and Lord) to exhorting his readers to do three things: *remember* the apostles' predictions of scoffers, *remain* in the love of God, and *rejoice* in our Savior. In verses 17–19 he calls his readers to remember. He addresses them as "beloved." As a pastor-shepherd, Jude is concerned for the flock of God. He doesn't want them endangered by the false teachers in their midst who are dressed in sheep's clothing but inwardly are ravenous wolves that bear bad fruit (see Matt. 7:15–20).

He also doesn't want them to think that he stands alone in his judgment of the ungodly. He calls them to remember the predictions of Christ's apostles. By pointing toward previous revelation, he continues to do what he has done in the previous verses. Furthermore, he grounds his readers in the faith that had been delivered to the saints by the apostles' teaching (see v. 3). The apostles predicted that there would be scoffers in the days between Christ's first and second comings (see Acts 20:29–30; 1 Tim. 4:1–3; 2 Tim. 3:1–5; 4:3–4; 1 John 2:18–22). These scoffers would follow their own ungodly passions instead of the way of the Lord. The Lord had previously predicted such scoffers would arise and lead many astray (see Matt. 24:11, 23–24).

Just as Jude had described the ungodly scoffers in the previous section of his letter (see vv. 8, 10, 12, 16), so now he uses three phrases to describe them. First, they are sensual. Instead of exhorting the brethren to strive toward holiness, they perverted the grace of God into sensuality. Second, they are divisive. Instead of bringing unity to the brethren based on their common salvation, they crept in unnoticed and caused division by introducing a false gospel. Finally, they are devoid of the Spirit. Far from worshiping, working, and witnessing in the Spirit's power, they worshiped their own gospel, worked at dividing the people of God, and perverted the church's witness to a watching world.

We also would be wise to remember the truth about scoffers. It seems that we have forgotten that ungodly people will creep into churches and distort the truth. Surely we are not less immune than those of Jude's day! We must be on our guard, saturated in the Scriptures, so that we can recognize error. Reading Scripture and hearing the preaching of the Word are means of grace God has given us to help us grow in holiness and to comfort us as we live on this side of glory. The Word of God is a gift to us. Study of God's Word should never become duty, but should be a delight to our souls. Our study of Scripture will prepare us to be eager examiners of the preaching, teaching, and writing going on in the church today. I hope the following questions will help you be an eager examiner of what you hear, see, and read (see Acts 17:11):

- Does this teaching exalt the triune God instead of exalting man?
- Is the authority of Scripture left uncompromised and unquestioned?
- Is the gospel at the center of the teaching?
- Is the teaching edifying?
- Does the teaching lead to repentance and renewal?
- Does the teaching encourage a life of holiness by God's grace?
- Does it examine everything through a biblical worldview?
- Does it accept the ordinary means of grace (the Scriptures, the sacraments, and supplication) as the primary way God sanctifies us?

- Is legalistic, moralistic, and therapeutic teaching rejected and Christ-centered teaching accepted?

- Are individualism and isolationism rejected and the covenant community accepted?

- Does it reject "need theology" ("I need this in order to be satisfied")?

- Does it teach that eternity is our hope instead of teaching our best life is now?

- Does it make our relationship with Christ, rather than rules and rituals, central?

- Are subjective experiences and emotions grounded in objective truth?

As we ask these questions, we will discover that there is much teaching, writing, speaking, and preaching that does not glorify God and make Christ preeminent. At the same time, the Lord has always preserved the truth and raised up proclaimers of it in each generation, bringing His story of salvation to pass. Let us join the efforts of those proclaiming the true grace of God and exalting our Master and Lord, Jesus Christ.

## II. A Call to Continue in the Faith: Remain (vv. 20–23)

In the previous verses, Jude exhorted us to remember the apostles' predictions of scoffers. Now he exhorts us to remain in the love of God. As those who are "sanctified by God the Father, and preserved in Jesus Christ" (v. 1) and who serve the God "who is able to keep [us] from stumbling" (v. 24), we are to "keep [ourselves] in the love of God" (v. 21). This is another example in Scripture of the imperative (what we are to do) intricately connected to and dependent upon the indicative (what God has already done for us).

Jude presents three ways we are to keep ourselves in the love of God. First, we are to build ourselves up in our most holy faith. The Lord has given us the means of grace to do so. We sit underneath the preaching of God's Word in community every Sunday and privately study the Scriptures each day. We partake of the sacraments (baptism and the Lord's Supper). We pray corporately and individually. And we engage in fellowship with our brothers and sisters in Christ.

Second, we are to pray in the Holy Spirit. Paul reminds us that we don't know how to pray as we ought, but that the Holy Spirit intercedes for us in prayer, according to the will of God. We can rest assured, then, that all things work together for good in our lives, if we love Him and are called according to His purpose (see Rom. 8:26–28).

Third, we are to look for the mercy of our Lord Jesus Christ that leads to eternal life. Our hope is anchored in the past (Christ's life, death, resurrection, and ascension); secured in the present (Christ our mediator constantly intercedes for us); and is looking in faith toward the future (Christ is coming again to save those eagerly waiting for Him). We will rejoice on the day of Christ's return because our judge and Savior is merciful. We have nothing to fear of His judgment because we are clothed in His righteousness. He has already atoned for our sins.

Jude exhorts us to handle those in our midst who are entangled in false teaching in three different ways, and we are to respond in these ways because of the mercy we have so graciously received from Christ. First, we are to have compassion on those who doubt. Those who have been shown compassion should extend compassion. Instead of judging those who are wrestling with whether a teaching is true or false, we are to lovingly, patiently, and perseveringly contend for the truth.

Second, we are to save some by pulling them out of the fire. There will be people in our midst who are flirting with the fire of false doctrine. We are to rescue them from the flames by pointing them to the true grace of God and to our Master and Lord, Jesus Christ. Jude draws his imagery from Zechariah 3, a passage he has already alluded to earlier (see v. 9). The context of Zechariah 3 is the heavenly courtroom. Satan is accusing Joshua the high priest, and the Lord is defending him. The Lord's defense is based only on the righteousness of the promised Branch, God's servant, which is fulfilled in Jesus Christ. In the Lord's rebuke to Satan he calls Joshua "a brand plucked from the fire" (Zech. 3:2). In other words, although Joshua deserved judgment, the Lord God extended grace to him based on the righteousness of the coming Branch, Jesus. Although we can't rescue others from the fire of judgment, the Lord uses us to proclaim grace and mercy and truth to them, exhorting them to return to holy living so that they will be restored to fellowship with the Lord and His people.

Third, we are to show mercy with fear to those whose garments are defiled by the flesh, most likely a specific reference to sexual sin. Rescue operations are dangerous. Ask any firefighter and he or she will tell you how easy it is to be burned by the flames of a raging fire if one is not properly clothed and equipped. If we are involved in a rescue mission, there is good reason to fear lest we be burned (tempted) with the same sin we are trying to save another person from. Jude continues to draw his imagery from Zechariah 3 in this verse. Joshua the high priest was clothed in filthy garments, but the Angel of the Lord told those who stood before Him to remove them so that He could clothe Joshua with clean ones (Zech. 3:4). Such "rich robes" pointed forward to the clothing Christ would give God's people. All those who flee the fire of sin and run to Christ will be welcomed by their Savior and gathered into His merciful arms.

As we undergo rescue operations, we need to suit up like a firefighter in proper clothing and equipment. Scripture tells us what clothing and equipment we need. Paul, addressing the saints in Ephesus, exhorted them to put on the full armor of God so that they would be able to stand against the schemes of the devil (Eph. 6:10–20). Too often we forget that we are in a wrestling match against the rulers, authorities, cosmic powers over this present darkness, and spiritual forces of evil in the heavenly places. Such forgetfulness is costly; it causes us to slip in places we need to stand firm. Thankfully, the Word of God does not leave us without a battle plan. It tells us what we must do.

First, we must fasten on the belt of truth (Eph. 6:14). We fasten on the belt of truth when we sit under the preaching of God's Word on Sundays, when we read and study the Scriptures as individuals and families, and when we speak the truth in love to one another.

Second, we must put on the breastplate of righteousness (Eph. 6:14). We put on the breastplate of righteousness when we walk in holiness by grace.

Third, we must put on the readiness given by the gospel of peace (Eph. 6:15). We put on the readiness given by the gospel of peace when we live as servants of God, subjecting ourselves to others in all humility, so that others might see our good works and glorify God.

Fourth, we must take up the shield of faith (Eph. 6:16). We take up the shield of faith by putting our hope in God, knowing His promises are sure, and looking forward in hope to the consummation of His kingdom while obediently walking in the ways of the Word.

Fifth, we must take up the helmet of salvation (Eph. 6:17). We take up the helmet of salvation by recognizing who we are and whose we are. We have been chosen by God, our Creator and Redeemer, to be "a chosen generation, a royal priesthood, a holy nation, His own special people, that [we] may proclaim the praises of Him who called [us] out of darkness into His marvelous light" (1 Peter 2:9).

Finally, we must take up the "sword of the Spirit, which is the word of God" (Eph. 6:17). The author of Hebrews tells us that "the word of God is living and powerful, and sharper than any two-edged sword, piercing even to the division of soul and spirit, and of joints and marrow, and is a discerner of the thoughts and intents of the heart" (Heb. 4:12).

### III. A Call to Continue in the Faith: Rejoice (vv. 24–25)

In the previous verses, Jude has called us to remember the apostles' predictions concerning scoffers, and he has called us to remain in the love of God. Now he calls us to rejoice in our Savior. There is no better way to close a letter of exhortation than to fix readers' eyes on the Lord God. It is important to remember that apart from the exaltation of who God is and what He has done for us, exhortations in Scripture would leave us hopeless. You and I cannot fulfill God's commands apart from God's grace. We cannot contend for the faith, uphold the true grace of God, and exalt our Master and Lord, Jesus Christ, without the grace of God. So Jude fixes our eyes on our source of strength at the very end of his letter.

Jude begins by reminding us that God is able to keep us from stumbling. Though sin remains in us on this side of glory, we are no longer dominated by it. It really is true that God has given us everything we need to live a life of godliness (2 Peter 1:3). We don't conjure up our own strength or follow a list of rules perfectly. Instead, we look to the One who holds us in the grip of His grace.

Next, Jude reminds us that God is able to present us faultless before His glorious presence with great joy. When Christ comes again we will have joy, because we will be robed in His righteousness and therefore able to stand in the presence of our Father with the joy of being His children.

Finally, Jude leads us in praise. We are to exalt God as the one living and true God. This concept is rooted in the Old Testament. The Old Testament church confessed, "The LORD our God, the LORD is one!" (Deut. 6:4). We are also to exalt God the Father as Savior. This concept is rooted in the Old Testament as well. One of Moses's final words to Israel before his death was in the form of a song. In it he exalted the Lord God as the Rock of Israel's salvation (see Deut. 32:15).

We are to approach God the Father through Jesus Christ, His Son, the only Mediator through whom we can worship God. We are to ascribe to God both glory and majesty, as well as dominion and power. The triune God's glory and majesty and dominion and power are everlasting, encompassing the past, the present, and the future.

Such praise should result in one thing: a hearty "amen," which means "So be it!" or "It is indeed true!"[1] Unlike the ungodly scoffers, believers are to proclaim the truth of the grace of our God and acknowledge our only Master and Lord, Jesus Christ.

Unless you are a firefighter, you don't know the adrenaline rush my friend's husband experiences as the fire truck races toward the raging fire in the middle of the night. But you may have experienced helping someone say no to addiction or despair, sensuality or distorted truth. Regardless of our occupations, we are all firefighters in the kingdom, called to proclaim the true grace of God and exalt our Master and Lord, Jesus Christ, as we extinguish the flames of the flesh and the Enemy in both our own lives and the lives of others. May the One who is able to keep us from stumbling and to present us faultless in His presence help us as we seek to fight well for His glory.

---

1. Green, *Jude & 2 Peter*, 137.

# Processing It Together...

1. What do we learn about God in Jude verses 17–25?

2. How does this reshape how we should view our present circumstances?

3. What do we learn about God's Son, Jesus Christ?

4. How should this impact our relationship with God and with others?

5. What do we learn about God's covenant with His people?

6. How are we to live in light of this?

7. How can we apply Jude verses 17–25 to our lives today and in the future?

8. How should we apply these verses in our churches?

9. Looking back at "Put It in Perspective" in your personal study questions, what did you find challenging or encouraging about this lesson?

10. Looking back at "Principles and Points of Application," how has this lesson impacted your life?

# Bibliography

Carson, D. A., and Douglas J. Moo. *An Introduction to the New Testament.* Reprint, Grand Rapids: Zondervan, 2005.

Clowney, Edmund. *The Message of 1 Peter.* The Bible Speaks Today. Downers Grove, Ill.: InterVarsity, 1988.

Davids, Peter H. *The Letters of 2 Peter and Jude.* The Pillar New Testament Commentary. Grand Rapids: Eerdmans, 2006.

Green, Gene L. *Jude & 2 Peter.* Baker Exegetical Commentary on the New Testament. Grand Rapids: Baker Academic, 2008.

Jobes, Karen H. *1 Peter.* Baker Exegetical Commentary on the New Testament. Grand Rapids: Baker Academic, 2005.

Johnson, Dennis E. *Him We Proclaim: Preaching Christ from All the Scriptures.* Phillipsburg, N.J.: P&R, 2007.

Köstenberger, Andreas J., and Richard D. Patterson. *Invitation to Biblical Interpretation: Exploring the Hermeneutical Triad of History, Literature, and Theology.* Invitation to Theological Studies Series. Grand Rapids: Kregel, 2011.

*The Westminster Confession of Faith and Catechisms.* The Orthodox Presbyterian Church, 2007.